2007
BLOOMING TWIG BOOKS
NEW YORK

BLOOMING TWIG BOOKS'
BOOK PUBLISHING BIBLE

*A Comprehensive Guide
to Self-Publishing*

FEATURING A COMPLETE TUTORIAL TO PODCASTING
AND A QUICK START GUIDE TO PUBLISHING

Compiled and Edited by

KENT S. GUSTAVSON

The Humane Publisher's Publishing Bible
Copyright ©2007 by Kent S. Gustavson
Blooming Twig Books LLC

Published by:

Blooming Twig Books LLC
3A Detmer Road
East Setauket, NY 11733
www.bloomingtwigbooks.com

ISBN 978-1-933918-18-1

DEDICATED TO:
Aspiring Authors Everywhere

CONTENTS OF THE PUBLISHING BIBLE

QUICK START PUBLISHING GUIDE

Determine Realistic Budget

Decide what your maximum budget is, and then work within that... Remember, spend one dollar on marketing for every dollar spent on publishing! Be realistic.

Don't bank on earning more money than you invest... Always leave yourself a way out!

Final Editing

Before you send your manuscript into any publisher, you should always give it to friends and family to look at and work on... After that, you still would do well to hire a professional to comb through the book for typos and coherency of content. This is the most important step in the publishing process! It is, after all the story that you are selling... The rest of the package just points to the text. Make it perfect!

Cover Design and Artwork

You CAN indeed judge a book by its cover. Or, perhaps the book-reading public just thinks they can... Most book buyers spend only a few seconds with your book before they pick up the next! If your cover design doesn't "pop," you will lose the public's attention!

Hire someone you believe will do good work on your concept! Don't be cheap, but also don't fall for schemes that attempt to get you to pay thousands for design work! (Cover design is included with most Blooming Twig Books Packages!)

Interior Layout Design

A step all too many authors pass up is layout design! When a customer picks up your book, and turns through it for 3 or 4 seconds, they will get an impression of your writing. Not from the words, as we might think, but from the DESIGN. Look at your favorite books, and you will see that all of them were painstakingly layed out! Again, this is an option you could pay thousands for, but can usually find a good deal on. (Layout Design is included with most Blooming Twig Books Packages)

Book Printing

Remember, when approaching the publishing process, that book printing is only a small aspect. Of course, physical copies of books are your ultimate goal, and what you will sell... But if you don't have a professionally layed-out, designed and edited product, bookstores and distributors will hesitate to stock your product!

Once you do get to printing, think about whether you are more concerned about quantity or quality. Quality will get you far more good reviews and press. Quantity will get you more profit, but only if you are able to sell them, which takes marketing!...

To chat with us about the unlimited options available to authors, call us at 1-866-389-1482.

Book Sales

When approaching selling your book in the new, expanded book market, you will need to cover as many fronts as you can! That means, submitting your book to local bookshops, getting book distribution (see next point), having your books for sale at many bookstores online, and, most importantly, from your personal website, and when you make appearances (signings and readings). You can, indeed, control your own sales entirely, and reap all of the benefits immediately! Call us for more information on the possibilities at: 1-866-389-1482

Book Distribution

Book distribution is the "real deal." A company, on your behalf, gets your books into stores! There could be no greater honor for an author... We can help you look for a distribution deal, but, again, quality is imperative for success in this!

Book Marketing/Promotion

There are many possibilities for book marketing, from inexpensive to costly. The thing to keep in mind is NOT to exceed your maximum budget! Never invest money that can't be recouped in some way...

And be careful to target a niche audience that will respond well to your marketing, advertising and promotion! Blooming Twig Books has a marketing package that can be customized, based on an author's needs, and their budget!

Choose Blooming Twig Books Author Packages for all of the above services and more...

Call 1-866-389-1482, or email: info@bloomingtwigbooks.com!

PREFACE

Most authors come to self-publishing as a "back-up plan..." Either exhausted by the search for a publisher or agent, or discouraged by the impersonal industry, authors decide to take their own careers in hand, and start looking for independent publishing options.

What many authors who go through this process might not know is that self-publishing is actually far more lucrative, and more likely to carve out a career for them than the traditional "publishing deal" they might have originally been seeking!

A good number of the books that major publishers produce go straight into the basement of the publishing house for long term storage, locked away from the light of day!

The industry is designed to only support the lucky, letting the rest of their books drop out of the bottom (if not successful)...

However, at the same time as the industry has become more and more difficult to break into, a brand new world of opportunity has opened up for independent publishers and authors. It is now possible for these often marginalized authors to "walk on" within the industry (pardon the reference to college athletics!).

If you do "make it" with a traditional publisher, what can you look forward to?

> Lots of contracts, signing away your percentages.
> An author tour with the sales benefiting the publisher, not your career.
> If your book doesn't sell (as is the case with 4 out of 5 authors signed to major publishers), it sits in the basement, and you have nothing, until the contract expires, when you are allowed legally to re-publish.

If you self-publish, what can you look forward to?

Complete control of every aspect of your book, sales, and
promotion.
100% of profits.
A book that is completely YOU…

Traditional Publishing	Self-Publishing
Become a "Well-Known" Author.	Not as easy to reach broad audience.
9 out of 10 books gather dust in the publisher's basement.	You control each and every book.
"What sells" is most important.	YOUR story is most important.
Author tour is booked by publisher (or neglected!)	You choose your tour dates, you hire your publicist!
Publisher pays for printing and artwork.	Author pays for printing and artwork.
Publisher earns the lion's share of the profit.	Author earns all profit.
Mainstream publishers are overloaded with inquiries.	The options for independent authors are ever expanding!
Traditional publishers are turning less profit each year.	Independent publishers are more and more successful.

Contact Blooming Twig Books to talk about all of your
self-publishing options. Call us Toll Free: 1-866-389-1482

INTRODUCTION

Blooming Twig Books LLC provides this reference book as a service to authors, no strings attached. And, as a further step, we are available to offer MORE advice about the industry and your project, problems, concerns, hopes, fears…

Of course, we also provide a great number of services, and would love to walk you through all possible options for your book. Page through this book, and see what we have to offer, and then be in touch!

Visit our website at **www.bloomingtwigbooks.com** for more information. In the meantime, we wish you all the best of luck in your publishing venture and adventure!

And, most importantly, have fun! Enjoy your new career as a published author!

Contact us anytime.

Kent Gustavson,
Operating Manager
Blooming Twig Books LLC

3A Detmer Road
East Setauket, NY 11733
Tel: 1-866-389-1482
Fax: 1-631-389-2607

Email: info@bloomingtwigbooks.com
Website: www.bloomingtwigbooks.com

Part One:
SELF-PUBLISHING

Tip #1

You CAN seem to be something you're not!
Choose a moniker! Come up with a name and logo for your faux "independent publisher" – it helps sales if your customers see a publisher's logo on the back!

Tip #2

Don't look for CHEAP, look for INEXPENSIVE.
There are plenty of options out in the industry at all price levels... Don't be discouraged by a limited budget!

Tip #3

Do your RESEARCH! All it takes is your favorite engine...
Get the low down on your competitors, find the best prices, tons of free advice and much more! Spend a few days at it.

Tip #4

Go with your GUT not your HEART!
Remember, this is business. Protect yourself! If you feel you are getting a shady deal, be careful! (Don't trust your heart)

Tip #5

ALWAYS sleep on it!
Take an extra day to think about every contract... Read every word, talk to your friends and family. THEN go for it!

For more information on Blooming Twig Books' Author Packages, call us today! 1-866-389-1482

CHAPTER 1
Book Printing

Note Print on Demand is not included in this chapter.
Refer to Chapter Two for more information.

Tip #1

ALWAYS establish your MAXIMUM spending limit first!
Look at your finances and make sure not to bet the bank...
Make moderate investments in your project, and once you
have proven success, invest more heavily...
Prove results first!

Tip #2

Think about spending ONE DOLLAR on marketing
for every dollar spent on publishing.
You will be far more successful!

Tip #3

Do you really need 10,000 copies of your book?
Try test printing a few hundred copies first!
It's a smart idea!

Tip #4

Remember, books DON'T sell themselves!
But they DO sell their AUTHOR. Put yourself into the book,
and think about creating an author tour and website!
Personal appearances really drive sales of your book!

Tip #5

QUALITY is the most important!!
Think quality first, and quantity later! Print a few hundred
copies of a beautiful book that will sell on any bookshelf...
Then go back and order the big numbers... No need to print
that many books before there is a demand for them!

Printer vs. Publisher

You'll be amazed what a PUBLISHER can do with the book you already thought was perfect!

A PRINTER can also put a great face on your book. But, they can only print what you send!

To compare the difference between a printer and a publisher, print out your book from your own printer, using Microsoft Word or another word processor. Then pull a copy of your favorite new book from your shelf, or look in a library or bookstore. Look at the margins, the fonts, the little flourishes (such as headers and dividers) within the professionally published books. Then look at the bland flavor of your printout.

This is an easy fix for any professional layout artist! Along with cover design and copy editing, interior layout design can truly make or break your book on the shelves of a bookstore, where your book will be competing with all of the major titles!

Hold your book to the highest standard. That doesn't mean you have to spend a fortune... But it does mean that you have to think critically and creatively, in order to get your manuscript and your final book into ship shape!

The printer can print only what you send. Make your book so beautiful inside and out that they will keep a copy on hand and show it to others! You will find that an attractive book will do great marketing for itself, simply by word of mouth (and email, of course!).

Choose printing options carefully!

PAPER

Cover Weight (Paper Thickness)
If your paper is too thin, your book will seem cheap.
If it's thicker, the printing will be more expensive.

Cover Color
White is the standard color, but other colors are possible.
Remember that most covers are printed in full color –
if you add colored paper to the mix, you might not know
what you'll get -- make sure you get a proof made!

Interior Weight (Paper Thickness) **
Novel-pulp
60 lb coated
60 lb uncoated
70 lb coated
70 lb uncoated
80 lb coated
80 lb uncoated
**Paper grade is also an important factor. There are
several grades of paper, from high to low quality.
(Always choose medium or high quality paper! It really
makes a difference!)

Interior Color
White (bright)
Cream (very elegant)
Natural (possibly recycled)

PAGE SIZE

4x7   Pulp trade paperback size
6x9   Trade paperback standard size
8 ½ x 11 Workbook size
Many other custom sizes are available
Special options such as die-cutting are available
(for custom shapes)

PRINTING HUES

Color Printed Cover
Other options are available, but uncommon.

Color Printed Interior
Color printed interior pages add a great deal of expense to your book. Adding a middle insert section is one way of handling this – with perhaps 12 or 18 color pages. That adds a minimal cost to printing. A completely color interior might become expensive, depending on the number of pages, and the number of copies printed. Think about your purchasing audience, and whether color is necessary. Black and white or 2-color pages are far less expensive!

Black/White or 2-Color Interior
Black and White interior pages are by far the most common, and the most reasonable in price. 2-color pages are possible, and might be a good alternative to color printing for a children's book or other book that needs a little extra flair!

BINDING

Hard Cover
Full color printed hard cover
Cloth bound hard cover
Cloth bound and embossed hard cover
      With full color, coated book jacket
      With 2-color, coated book jacket
Other options are available

Trade Paperback
Perfect Binding (paperbacks are perfect bound)
Saddle Stitched (for smaller books and pamphlets)
Covers can be printed on both sides, or just one side

Custom Options are always available! Put a CD inside the back cover, get the book cut to a specific shape, etc...

TRADITIONAL PRINTING ROUTES

CHILDREN'S BOOKS

Children's hardcover books are very expensive to produce at quantities under a thousand. The reason for that is that digital presses just haven't developed a method for creating the books cheaply. There are a number of options to create paperback books, or limited color hardcovers in order to reduce price... Or, simply order a thousand or more copies!

The traditional route to publishing a children's book involves very high quality scanning, and professional layout design inside of the book. The cover should also be carefully spaced and layed out... Then, the books are sent to print.

It is imperative that you get a proof made for the book, so that you can see it on the actual paper, etc., before you get hundreds or thousands made, and find a mistake, or color discrepancy!

HARDCOVER BOOKS

The most common way for traditional publishers to release new books in their catalogs has been to first release a hardcover, and, a few months later, release a softcover trade edition.

This carries over into high-end self-publishing. And one of the only ways that traditional publishers pick up on independently published books for their catalogs is when they see measured success of a self-published hardcover edition. When the success has already been proven, the traditional publishers all come calling!

Hardcovers cost a great deal more than trade paperbacks, so they are not the best option for every author. But they sell at a much higher price than paperbacks, and can therefore sometimes be a much better investment.

Authors usually find the price per copy of printing the most important. Hardcover books become much more affordable upwards of a thousand copies because of offset printing. Below a thousand copies, digital presses are the most reasonable.

Most self-published and independently published authors see little need to publish their books in hardcover, because their level of investment is small. Trade paperbacks are, in most cases, the most reasonable and prudent way to start the process of publication.

TRADE PAPERBACK BOOKS

The simplest, most widespread, accepted, and most inexpensive route to first-time publishing is trade paperbacks. Honestly, don't we all go to the paperback section first to see if the book we've been itching to read has been released yet in its cheaper form? Not wanting to pay nearly 30 bucks for the hardcover edition, an enormous number of readers love paperbacks, and flock to bookstores around the globe to purchase them!

The path to trade paperback publishing is fairly straightforward. Cover design and interior layout are key, because of the simplicity of the softcover medium. And the most important thing to keep in mind with paper quality is whether you want bleed-through or not. Check out a cheaply printed book and a more expensive one at your local bookstore. You will see that the inexpensive pulp edition of your favorite book bleeds through from page to page – you can see through the pages... It doesn't matter to the reader all that much, if they've committed to purchasing the cheapest edition of a book... But, if they were expecting to get a quality edition, they want it to look and feel the part! (So choose paper thickness wisely!)

Don't be afraid about what your market will think of paperbacks. They are the most marketable of all book editions. Now just think about getting that book cover and layout perfect! Blooming Twig Books LLC can help! Call us at 1-866-389-1482.

QUANTITY VS. QUALITY

ALWAYS UNDERESTIMATE YOUR SALES!

Prepare yourself for a nice surprise when you sell a single copy of your book to a stranger! Give copies to all of your loved ones, and sell a few to friends... And then be satisfied when you start to get your books out into the public sphere! It is a true joy.

Then, and only then, be concerned about the next step. The number one reason to be an author is for the joy of it. And the greatest pleasure always comes from giving a copy to your spouse, kids, mother, father, friend... It doesn't matter what Oprah might say, as long as mom loves it!

If you underestimate your sales, you will also prepare yourself for "failure," and turn it into something remarkable. A step in the right direction. Perhaps the next book needs more planning. Perhaps this book just needs more marketing. Maybe an author tour or distribution will drive more interest...

If you, instead, overestimate your sales, you run into big problems when it comes to making your money back! Instead of a joyful journey into authordom, it becomes a treacherous road of trying to make back your investment! It might take a year, or it might take ten... Don't do that to yourself!

SUGGESTIONS FOR PRINTING

PRINTING SUGGESTION #1

GO FOR IT, but be careful to have "perfection." If you order 1,000 or 10,000 copies, you'll have to live with your new book for years and years (inevitable mistakes included)!

You'll step into your closet, and you'll have to reach around a dozen big boxes to get to your clothes... You'll set foot into your basement, and you'll be waist deep in piles of books!

Get a test printing of 25 copies, or make a couple hundred. Give them away, sell a few, and see if people find any flaws...

Then, fix all the little mistakes the world finds, and print the thousands of copies you had been planning!

PRINTING SUGGESTION #2

Work on PERFECT interior layout, cover design, etc. Insist upon absolute perfection from yourself and all of the people working on your book!

Then print 500, ten thousand, however many you like! But make very, very sure that there are no flaws before going to press!

MOST IMPORTANT

You are creating YOUR OWN image for the world.
Don't settle for anything BUT professional!

Let us help you! Call us toll free at 1-866-389-1482.

CHAPTER 2
Print On Demand

PRINT ON DEMAND
PROS & CONS

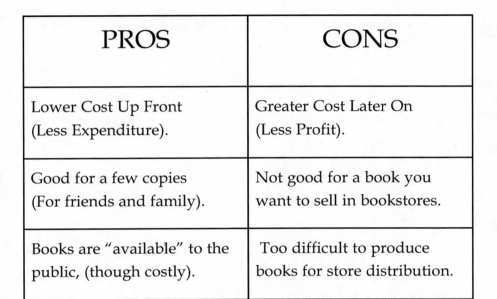

PROS	CONS
Lower Cost Up Front (Less Expenditure).	Greater Cost Later On (Less Profit).
Good for a few copies (For friends and family).	Not good for a book you want to sell in bookstores.
Books are "available" to the public, (though costly).	Too difficult to produce books for store distribution.
Cheaper.	Lower Quality.

Print on Demand is a great idea for hobbyists. Not for authors.

Take control of your publishing! If you self-publish, you
OWN your books. YOU own your rights. No small
percentages to pay to anyone... Ask the questions,
and you will draw your own judgment!

SAVE MONEY, DON'T P.O.D.!

P.O.D.	Self-Publishing
Good for less than a hundred copies.	Good for any number of copies.
Little or no initial investment required.	Requires initial investment (200 dollars to thousands)
The POD company takes $$ for each copy sold.	You own everything. Much larger profits.
Few, if any, author copies.	All of the copies are yours, to sell and use for promotion.
Not having author copies reduces distribution.	Giving copies to media greatly increases sales.
Nearly impossible to get professional distribution.	All forms of distribution and publicity are very successful.
Dependent on POD company for every copy.	Independence. Embarking on new career. You're the boss.

PRINT ON DEMAND SUMMARY

Don't do P.O.D.!
Don't use Print on Demand unless you are a hobbyist, and want to sell or give away 100 or fewer copies of your book...

We have heard story after story about the disappointments caused by P.O.D. Don't waste your time with something that appears cheap, and in fact only steals the value of your work! Print with confidence, and you will be lauded by the press and the public!

Print on Demand might be a great technology, and it is great when you want a few copies of your book. But what you don't see on the surface is that it's just another way for the printing industry to make a buck off of you, the author!

The Print on Demand publishers take a fee from you to set up your book. Then they take a fee each time they produce a book for you. You are never "in the clear." You always owe someone something. The difference between that and Self-Publishing is that, if you self-publish your books, YOU are in control. And you sell the books until you have made back your investment. At that point, every book you sell is just frosting. Each book is in the profit column. That's part of the fun of this business!

AND, in order to self-publish, you don't need to publish 5,000 books. You only need to publish a few. Don't think that only the POD firms are able to print small numbers of books! Digital technology has become the key to independent publishing! If you can afford a modest sum, digital presses can print anywhere from 1-500 copies of your book affordably... Blooming Twig Books works with a number of these presses, and can help you think about all self-publishing options.

Take publishing into your own hands! Don't P.O.D.!
You need author copies of your book in order to do signings, readings, to get press and distribution for your book. If you self-publish, you can have many books for marketing and publicity!

If you have questions, or would like to tell us your "horror story" related to P.O.D., please be in touch! We will always listen... We would also love to tell you about all options and possibilities for self-publishing, controlled by you... With the benefits all gathered by you, the author!

Call us toll free at 1-866-389-1482 to chat about all of your options for book printing and publishing!

CHAPTER 3
E-Books

TIP #1

Use E-Books for Promotion!
Give out e-books freely as promotion, to targeted media contacts, to supporters, to reviewers…

TIP #2

Send an E-Book to Investors…
…to help pay for publication, printing and marketing. (And send them a copy of the "real" book upon release.)

TIP #3

Give a TASTE of the E-Book…
…on your website and/or in emails… Then tell them where to buy the rest! Blooming Twig Books can help you set up e-book purchasing directly on your website!

TIP #4

Submit your E-Books to Online Sites Just Like Yours.
Find sites of authors just like you, and sites that might be responsive to your book, or your story, and contact them… Tell them you'd like to send a free e-book for their perusal.

TIP #5

Send E-Books to Every Reviewer.
You have to GIVE free stuff in order to RECEIVE! Don't be afraid to be generous… You will find that reviewers and others will be very helpful and supportive in return!

There are many varieties of E-books, from simple to complex!

You only pay once!

With a little investment, never again pay for printing! Whether you sell fifty copies or fifty thousand, you will never again pay to create and set up the e-book! (Unlike trade books that you pay for again and again…)

E-Books are also fantastic marketing tools.

It is highly effective to give away a little of the e-book as promotion, for free, online, through emails, on your website, and so on… Once you have people hooked, you have them purchase the rest: At the end of the free section, they will absolutely have to keep reading, and they will follow the prompt to purchase the book!

About the Various Types of E-Books

MOST COMMON E-BOOKS

The most common e-books on the market are PDF-based e-books. There are several varieties, and thousands of ways to obtain and purchase them, and they are by far the easiest to navigate, the most universal, and the most practical form of e-book. Unfortunately, PDF e-books are also the easiest to "bootleg" and send to friends and family, harmlessly thinking that the PDF copy of a book is just like a physical copy of a book, where you can pass it on... So, there is a big trade-off here. The easiest to use e-book is also the easiest to steal, and will probably lead to quite a bit of lost income. After all, the people that (illegally) send the PDF to one another are the same people that would otherwise have referred someone else to a bookstore online to purchase the e-book!

SAFEST E-BOOKS

The safest e-books for the author are the ones that include security features that limit "bootlegging." Blooming Twig Books builds secure e-books that use Flash technology, and if unzipped by the customer, cannot be shared from one user to another, though just as easy to use, if not more so, than the run-of-the-mill PDF e-books. Although the user can print the individual chapters using their own home printer, they can only view the e-book on an internet browser (though they don't need to be connected to the internet). If a purchaser wants to send a copy of the Flash e-book to a friend (illegally), the friend won't be able to open up the files within the e-book, because it will register as corrupted. For more information on these attractive, safe e-books, contact Blooming Twig Books at 1-866-389-1482.

There are many other "safe" e-books offered on the web, and elsewhere, and many of them are very handy and convenient. However, most of them require you to download some software or another in order to view their particular e-books. The Blooming Twig Books Flash E-Books don't require any special downloads, and are viewed much as a website would be, though no internet connection is required.

LEAST SAFE E-BOOKS

For the consumer, of course there are also many concerns about the downloading of products from the web. The most dangerous of these is the one pertaining to .exe (self-executing) files. Many ebooks are downloaded as these .exe files – they run as little programs, and once deleted, they disappear as quickly as they showed up! But, .exe files also are the best way for spyware and viruses to attack consumers' computers, so many users shy away from .exe file e-books (with due cause!).

How to Sell & Market E-Books

There are many ways to set up e-book sales on the web. Here, we present two approaches. If you are curious about more possibilities, give us a call at 1-866-389-1482.

<u>Simplest Way to set up E-Book Sales:</u>

You send the e-book to someone who orders your product directly from your website, by telephone, by mail, or by e-mail. You can send the e-book to them on a home-burned CD, by e-mail, or it can be somewhere online, and you forward your customer the address of the file online.

The pluses:

Very simple to set up... You likely already have the tools to make this work! If you have a website, simply write the information up there, then have people email you their orders. The purchases could also be made via paypal or another processor on your website that is fairly simple to set up.

The minuses:

You will lose a lot of customers with the requirement that they be in touch with you. Most internet customers want to purchase books quickly and easily with their credit card! Also, if your e-book finds success, it will be a lot of work sending them out! Your customers must have a very large email account for an ebook that has pictures, or, alternatively, if you store the e-book online for them to download, if it's not in an encrypted location, they can just tell their friends where the link is, and anyone can download it (illegally) with no trouble at all!

Best Way to set up E-Book Sales:

Host the e-books with a site such as Blooming Twig Books. People order the books securely with their credit card, then download the files directly to their home machine. If they have any trouble, they get in touch with that store. Then you get a check in the mail when the e-books have sold.

The pluses:

All of the customer service aspects are taken care of for you. You also don't have to actually send out copies of the e-book: the website that sells them for you does all of that automatically... You are simply notified when you sell a book!

The minuses:

You will have to pay whatever store sells your ebooks a small cut of the profits. At the Blooming Twig Books store, we ask for $4.00 of each sale, whether an actual book or an e-book. Other stores sell based on a percentage – they will likely take 30-60 percent of your sale price.

CHAPTER 4
Cover Design/Other Artwork

Tip #1
DON'T trust your own eye!
Even the best artists ask others their opinions, and
(with with great annoyance at times) take the new ideas
into consideration. Choose your MOST critical friend,
and take their opinion FIRST... Most friends will only
tell you what they think you want to hear!

Tip #2
A little work can go a long way...
In deciding where to spend money on a book publishing
project, the most vital part is the cover. This is TRULY the
place the book is judged. Of course, once the reviewer or
reader has gotten past the cover, they will also judge the
interior for quality... But they have to get there first! Look
at your favorite books in the library, your home, or at your
corner bookstore. They are BEAUTIFUL inside and out!

Tip #3
The cover WILL sell your book!
Trust us. On your website or on a shelf,
your cover choice can really influence sales!

Tip #4
Don't Spend Thousands of Dollars just because...
a cover artist has a nice advertisement or has done someone
else's cover well! Look at what they could do for your project (But there's no need to overspend to get a good cover!)

Tip #5
Contract for the PROJECT, not by the HOUR.
Ask about all hidden fees, and, if you are paying by
the hour, make sure you trust the artist's work ethic!
Most good artists will do projects for a certain
fee (that's usually also negotiable!)

COVER DESIGN

VISIBILITY

The most important thing is for your cover to have good visibility and legibility, whether you make it very small or very large. You want the design to be catchy, but not distract from the title of the book, or your name. The title must be large, and readable, so that if you get a review in a magazine, it will still be clear at a very small size, or in black and white.

INDUSTRY STANDARDS

Look around in bookstores, in libraries, and on your own bookshelves. What is the industry standard for book covers? Which ones stand out to you? What book would you simply HAVE to pick up while walking through the aisles at your favorite bookshop? Or if you were surfing on the internet, what book cover (even in a very small size) would attract your attention? Covers have a great deal to do with the current trends, as well as a combination of getting the idea across, being unique, and still traditional!

KEY INFORMATION

Sometimes it's hard to pack all of your information into a small cover... It's imperative that you get ENOUGH information across, but it's very difficult to do it while still looking beautiful! That's something a professional can do a great deal to help you with... If you are designing on your own, at least make your titles big, and your subtitles small, concise and clear. Aesthetically, work on all attention going towards the large title. The subtitle, or small description, is only for those that wish to find out more... Most people won't look at that at first.

UNIQUE

Of course, having a unique cover will lead to sales right off the bat (if your content and layout are also very high quality and look good). If your book stands out on any shelf, it will do its own marketing! Look around the shelves for the most unique books, and the ones that look just like all of the others! Then, you must make a decision about HOW unique to make the book, and in turn, how traditional to keep it. Tradition is also very important – people don't necessarily want to be shocked by a book. There is a fine line there! It depends on your genre...

TRADITIONAL

What is a traditional book cover? What are we comfortable with? What do we feel safe purchasing, for our children, for ourselves, for a gift, etc... Again, look for your favorite covers, of the books that you would love to sit near the fireplace with, curled up with a mug of tea. Traditional covers are simple, but quite effective. All book purchasers and readers are attracted not only by simplicity, but also certain colors, textures, shapes, etc. Look for all of those attributes in the books you love. Then use those elements in your own cover, along with unique elements in your design that will show freshness!

REMEMBER

You have less than 10 seconds to make your impression! In that 10 seconds, on the internet, on a bookshelf, or somewhere else, the customer will make their decision based on a massively complex system of factors, including design and artwork!

Be in touch with us for all of your design needs! 1-866-389-1482

CHILDREN'S BOOK ILLUSTRATION

The most important part of a children's book (though the story is also extremely vital) is the artwork. If you are planning to illustrate your own book, read below. Or, there are thousands of illustrators out there to work on your book with you. Of course, if you have contact to a well-known children's illustrator, that adds some bonus points to your book from the beginning. However, it is not necessary to have a well-known illustrator. On the contrary, it might be much more reasonable and unique to find your own illustrator. Perhaps you can find an artist that has not done this kind of work before, and is therefore very interested in working hard on your project! Another idea is to look for a student in a local university, and audition them... Guarantee them a small fee for one page, and then choose from several different students' work. You are bound to find one that will match your ideas! And you will save a bundle of money! Most students will be happy with a relatively modest wage. Offer to pay them a few hundred dollars for the entire project, or offer them fifty dollars per page... If you hire a professional illustrator, you might pay thousands!

CONVERTING THE ARTWORK

Once you or your artist have completed the artwork, it is imperative that you scan the artwork into a graphic design program at the HIGHEST possible quality! Then, you will be able to manipulate, zoom, modify, even colorize it, change certain aspects, and add text later on... If you don't scan at the highest level, the book will look fuzzy to the reader, and you won't be able to change it afterwards unless you re-scan! If you don't have a high quality scanner, they can be relatively inexpensive at your local office store. Don't skimp on a few dollars if it means you are talking about your children's book! Get a very good scanner (they only cost around 100 dollars).

QUALITY

Be very careful, and concerned about the quality of the artwork, both in production and in upload. People will see every blemish, every fingerprint! Choose carefully who your illustrator is, and if it's you, then be careful to produce high quality artwork! And, when you scan the artwork in, make sure it remains at the top quality! And, when you decide on a printer, make sure that your printer has high quality printing options for your full color book. Some printers are not able to print as high quality as others. Many printers will offer to send you a sample of their work before you decide to work with them.

VARIED PRINTING OPTIONS

Because of the many available printing options for children's books, from hard to softcover, dust jackets, full color, 2-color, black and white, or die cut, etc. (see the printing chapters in this book), the artist you choose or process you use should depend heavily on those choices. The artist will also have to know all of the specifics before they begin designing the cover! Contact us if you have any questions about any of this! 1-866-389-1482.

CHILDREN'S BOOK INDUSTRY

The children's book industry is at the same time the most lucrative and the most difficult to get into! There is always a demand for children's books, and there always will be, for even after parents have stopped reading themselves, they will always purchase books for their children. And, there will always be schools, and those schools will always need books! However, at the same time, the industry is absolutely crowded with books. Every writer and all of their friends and family think that they will make a million bucks with their children's book. Find a niche market, and you might just achieve good success. But you will have to work at it! If your book is about nature, about death, or about school – look to those markets to sell your books! You will find success... Call us for more ideas: 1-866-389-1482.

CHAPTER 5
Interior Layout Design

Tip #1

Do everything YOU can do BEFORE outsourcing!
The more you do before you hire someone else to work
on your design, the more the design reflects your ideas!
If you work really hard, after all, you may not need
much assistance at all! Save thousands on
professional book layout that way!

Tip #2

Don't work on LAYOUT until EDITING is done...
The most important thing to remember with layout is that
you should have everything in stone before you begin!
It's okay to go back and make a few changes, but do
your best to get everything ship shape before working
on layout. Let your layout designer work on aesthetic,
and not have to worry about any editing aspects!

Tip #3

Microsoft Word layout is NOT enough!
Nine out of ten authors believe that their Microsoft Word
layout is either perfect, adequate, or somewhere in between.
They couldn't be more wrong! It's okay only for friends
and family! Look at all books for sale in your local
bookstore, and you will see the difference!

Tip #4

Be specific, but DEFER to your designer!
Would you tell a carpenter how to sand a board?
Probably not – you just tell them you want it smooth!
Let your designer do the creative work! Just be
specific about the aesthetic you want...

Tip #5

Don't be afraid to spend money (in the right places)...
The more you spend on appearance, the more chance your
book has to be successful. But, of course, you shouldn't
spend too much – so choose carefully where to spend!

THE DOWN-LOW ON LAYOUT

Most authors find professional layout design, or any sophisticated design, to be an unnecessary step in their process towards publication!

On the contrary! Interior layout design is probably the most crucial step towards a professional product!

Print out a page from your Microsoft Word program and compare it to your favorite book… Think about:

INSIDE MARGIN

The left and right margins are very important… Remember that, when you fold the book out to read it, you are losing a lot of space on the inside! (Try it with the nearest paperback, and you will see what we are talking about!) It is also vital that your margins not be ragged – we can tell you more about that as well as much more about the margin-setting process!

SPACING

Do you want your book double spaced? Single spaced with bigger words? Somewhere in between? How much space between paragraphs? This is something that might not matter much initially (especially when checking it out on a computer screen), but once you have printed the book, you will notice these little details (as will your customers)!

HEADERS

Take a look at your favorite books, and you will see that they all have unique header styles. (These are the words and page numbers at the top or bottom of the page) Not that any of them have to be extraordinary, but they have to help the overall feeling the book gives off... Having a professional work on your book will show you the power of headers! In the layout designer's bag of tricks, the headers are the icing on the cake...

COPYRIGHT PAGES

For those among you who are really excited to be among the ranks of the published, there is something about the copyright page that is quite satisfying. You put your copyright information there, your ISBN number, your name, address... But the best part is the statement that NOBODY is allowed to copy or re-distribute the book, without your permission! This is the final ownership page, where everyone goes to see who made this gorgeous book they just purchased at their local bookstore!

TITLES AND HEADINGS

By titles and headings, we mean any kind of bold, large, beautiful words at the start of a section, telling the reader where they are! These are like the road signs... Some books need more (just like some roads DEFINITELY need more!), and some are just easily navigable by themselves! Your signs have to be very useful and practical, but also attractive, and in some way **blink-in-your-face-attention-getting!!** Again, a designer can help you make this choice... Many authors make their titles either boring or pink-and-green-with-purple-polkadots gregarious! If you work on the titles yourself, try to make a tasteful choice in between... Again, take your tips from your favorite books!

FONT STYLE/SIZE

Another aspect of layout that few readers notice while perusing their newest piece of pulp fiction is the font style and size. The default fonts in the most popular layout programs are totally overused and should be avoided at all costs – they don't look unique whatsoever... And, the fonts that look like cursive, or are extra bubbly, curly, sharp, or something else are just a little to fancy to sell to a mainstream audience – they look 'cheap' or kitschy. Many book designers have a set of fonts that they like the best, from thin and elegant to dark and gregarious!... If you would like to experiment on your own with this, start subtly, and progress from there... Little differences are often the most effective!

REMEMBER!

You only have 10 seconds to hook your sale!

The most important aspects readers look for:

Beautiful, Unique Cover
Traditional Layout with little spicy differences
(in font, headers, dividers…)

This is your offspring in the world – clothe it only in the best you can afford (within your project's budget!)… Remember, people DO judge a book by its cover!!

Blooming Twig Books LLC offers interior layout design at no additional cost with every Standard Plus and Professional Plus Package, and can customize all of the options we listed above with you.

Even if you aren't sold on our package or our layout services, please give us a call with any of your questions!

Call us toll-free at: 1-866-389-1482.

CHAPTER 6
Copy and Content Editing

Tip #1

Do YOUR work first, and try to read CRITICALLY!

Editing your own manuscript can be the hardest thing in the world to do! Do your best to pretend you've never read it before, and be as hard on yourself as you can be!

Tip #2

Friends/Family

The easiest people to persuade to read, correct, and give you feedback on your book, are your close friends and family. Be sure to give them the go-ahead to read VERY critically, and to send you all of their feedback, so that you can make final revisions… Trade them a favor, or a free book once they're released!

Tip #3

Local Editor/Student

The most reasonable editor, once you've decided your book is ready for serious copy and content editing, is a local one, not one attached to a major publisher… Ask around among your friends and family, and you will likely find a great editor who won't charge you an arm and a leg! You might also want to ask a local graduate student or precocious undergraduate to work with you for a reasonable fee!

Tip #4

Have editor work WITH you, not FOR you…

Once you have decided to work with a professional editor, don't let the editor do all the work! Ask them to go back and forth with you, so that you have more control! That's what we do at Blooming Twig Books
Call us toll-free at 1-866-389-1482

Tip #5

Ask for CONTENT editing as well as COPY editing…

Because your content is the most important part of the book!

EVERY Top Author Has Editors!

EVERY top author has editors – great ones! They work on the manuscript with the author, back and forth, sometimes even brutally for a few months or a few years...

You might think, "That's for the famous authors, not for me..." Or perhaps you're in denial, and are telling yourself, "I've worked really hard on this book – I don't need any more editing... I'm ready to get it published..."

Remember two things. First, this book will be out there forever. Once you publish it, give it away, sell it, or anything else, your friends, family, and strangers will hang onto it forever (unless, God forbid, they sell it to the nearest thrift store!) Do a good job on it! Make sure it's as perfect as you can get it! It will always reflect directly on you! And second, the book can ALWAYS take more editing. The best authors in the world complain ceaselessly about how much work it is to publish... Because it's a brutal process, not unlike childbirth... And it seemingly never ends (like raising children)... Once the book is published, there's something else... marketing! And after that, if you have a successful book, what about the next book?

Editors can do wonders for books... You see it on the shelves every day. Every book you love has likely been polished by several editors... Just like every song you love has been produced in a studio, and just like your favorite films have probably been edited beautifully with expensive equipment!

Don't forget to set a spending limit... Although editing is highly important to the future and success of your book, it's not worth going over-budget beyond the point of no return!... And you might be able to get a professional looking book at a reasonable price in many different ways... For example, we at Blooming Twig Books LLC include editing in our Professional Plus Author Packages at no additional cost!

REMEMBER:

Make sure to do as much editing on your own, and without cost, as you can BEFORE outsourcing!

THEN choose a great editor, who is eloquent, interested in your book, and willing to work WITH you on copy editing and content editing!

Rely on family and friends throughout the process! They will help you out, encourage you, and make your book a great deal better with the comments they offer! And they will most likely do it all for free! (Nevertheless, recognition in your Acknowledgments section, and a free copy of the book would be a nice perk to offer them, as well!)

Blooming Twig Books LLC can help you with all of your editing issues! Call us toll-free at: 1-866-389-1482.

Part Two:
PUBLICITY

FOR EVERY DOLLAR YOU SPEND
ON PUBLISHING AND PRINTING, YOU MUST
SPEND ONE DOLLAR ON MARKETING
(IF YOU WANT A SUCCESSFUL RETURN)…

Tip #1

A little internet research goes a long way!
The cheapest, most effective, and most current research you can conduct is with your favorite search engine! Gather all kinds of information about your competitors: both authors and publishers… See what their books look like, and see where they sell them and market them.

Tip #2

Online presence does NOT mean traffic…
Online presence (website, blog, etc…) does not necessarily mean traffic. Your website is like your home address. Rarely do you ever see a traveling salesman anymore, just as you will find few unplanned visitors to your site! YOU need to drive the traffic!

Tip #3

Find your NICHE
In any kind of marketing, publicity or advertising you must figure out where your book FITS!… Take your new niche, and focus on that niche with all of your efforts. Once you find some success there, move into some other niches, and larger pools of potential buyers!

Tip #4

DON'T waste money on advertising…
Don't buy advertising space that hasn't been proven for authors! (Don't buy an ad in the New York Times just because it has a lot of circulation.) Don't believe what an advertising salesman might tell you, unless you've seen real possibility in what they're saying!

Tip #5

Start small, with great hopes!
Don't aim at Oprah – aim for local radio, and work your way up!

CHAPTER 7
Author Website

Tip #1

Don't choose a site until you weigh your options...
There are tons of places to get a web address,
domain name or web site, but most of them are difficult
to use, some are really inaccessible, and others are highly
dangerous for your content – hosted on servers alongside
pornography or worse! Ask us for advice before you
choose! Or at least do good background checks! And
you will get what you pay for, so watch out...

Tip #2

Look at your competitors' or favorite authors' sites...
No site is perfect... Look at your competitors'
or favorite authors' sites, and find their flaws, and
their strong points! Plan you own site out, thinking
about what you want the world to know about you!
Be original, but make sure to cover your bases!

Tip #3

What will your site be used for?
Who will be using your site? Will it be clients, readers,
colleagues, pastors, students? Cater your site directly
to them... Give them a special deal if they join your
newsletter or mailing list. Give them a special
peek inside the book, inside your life...

Tip #4

Do you want your personal data on the internet?
Important decision! Decide how much information you
want to share! If you include your email address, spammers
will find you. If you include your home address, maybe you
feel insecure about that... All of that is your choice!...

Tip #5

Ask people who know to help you out!
If you don't know anyone, contact us...
Call us toll free: 1-866-389-1482.

YOUR WEBSITE IS YOUR ADDRESS!

Authors NEED a website like a business needs an office address. Many years ago, just having an address meant that you would get salespeople knocking on your door. Those times are long past... Now, mass mailings and email have replaced those hard-working salespeople.

At the beginning of the internet, just having a website was enough to attract a great deal of attention. But now there are millions upon millions of websites out in cyberspace! Just BEING online doesn't drive people to your site, and bring in customers! You must put up a sign, hopefully on a major throughway... Then people will come visit your site... Whether your sign is a little cardboard one that says "garage sale" or a huge one that flashes, blinks and more, you are attempting to do the same thing with both. (Attract traffic!)

So, what is your billboard on the internet? Anything from the most expensive advertising to free recommendations... The best (and cheapest) way to get advertising for your site is to have others link to you...

Think about it this way. Before elections, politicians post their signs on street corners – the signs pile up, and there are often dozens of them to look at. This is good exposure for each, but is not often very effective for any of them. If instead the same candidate has 10 houses along a short stretch of roadway with individual signs in their yards, they are getting FAR better publicity, at a much smaller cost, and less crowding!

In the same way, you need to ask individual sites, ultimately with high online rankings, to add you to their links pages, or to do a review of your book. You will be amazed what a few recommendations can do for the web rankings of your own site!

BASIC WEBSITE

A modest website would contain about five to ten "pages" with simple information on them. You might include your biography, your book's information, an ordering page, a contact page, and perhaps a few more small sections about your book.

The modest website is something we recommend to ALL authors. With the low cost of maintenance, and a minimum of work required to set this up, it is a NECESSITY for your book, and for you! We all know that everyone goes home after an interview on the radio, or a reading in a bookstore, and types the book's title directly into their favorite search engine, trying to find out more, or get a special deal on the paperback. Don't let some other site take the traffic that was meant for you! Call us for help, toll free at: 1-866-389-1482.

Any time you have a review or other media attention, people will immediately find you and your products – and that is the ultimate goal, if you have a modest website… If you would like a highly organized, specific, content driven, and search engine listed site, you should consider spending an extra few dollars and investing in an author website, or a more advanced version of the basic website!

AUTHOR WEBSITE

As part of our Author Packages, we often include sites from our partner site AmericanAuthor.com – the premiere site for Author Websites. Their sites make it possible to create everything from an online press kit to an author newsletter, all from a simple online terminal with complete, simple tutorials! The entire site can be updated at any point by authors themselves, no fancy knowledge necessary – once you get the hang of it, it's just as easy as using your favorite word processing program! Check them out at www.americanauthor.com. Tell them Blooming Twig Books sent you, for special pricing. Or, purchase a Blooming Twig Author Package, and ask us to include one of their sites.

CUSTOM PROFESSIONAL WEBSITE

At Blooming Twig Books, we offer custom professional websites of every variety, from basic to Flash. If you want to go to the next level with your website, think about our custom professional sites! That means we work with you to design a handmade, unique site with any number of custom options!

Our Custom Professional Author Websites are much easier to transfer to another server at a later date, and much easier to upgrade to a new design, etc., if you need to update your look, or if you have published a new book, etc.

There are many other places online where you can find people or companies to design a custom website for you – and we encourage you to browse around… But come back to us if you are interested in a website custom designed for authors! We will work with you on the options that you need!

Be in touch with us if you are interested in a custom professional website: Toll-free 1-866-389-1482.

Websites aren't all that hard!

The entire online process is far simpler than you may think! You have done the REAL hard work, writing a complete book. We help you with the EASY work, designing a custom site with you to develop your WEB ADDRESS!

No fear necessary!

We walk you through each and every step... We make it easy for you!

Contact us today!
Call Us Toll-Free: 1-866-389-1482.

CHAPTER 8
Author Podcasting

Tip #1

Develop your IDENTITY!

Podcasters all have a unique online identity, directly related to their subject matter! Make your identity unique, intriguing, but also immediately identifiable to your audience!

Tip #2

Check out other PODCASTS for ideas!

The easiest way to figure out what to say on a podcast, how to program it, and what topics to try, is to check other podcasts out for ideas!... There are hundreds of podcast aggregators online, which collect these podcast "feeds" (or subscriptions), and play them all for you in one place… (Itunes is one popular podcast feed reader.) Once you have found a feed reader, you can download the podcasts directly to your mp3 player or a program on your home computer, and listen to them in their entirety.

Tip #3

Get comfortable with your equipment FIRST!

Before you jump out there and start putting your podcasts online, feel out the process, hone your own podcasting skills a few times, and then go for it!

Tip #4

Have show notes and post them online…

It is highly important to have show notes and post them online on your podcast feed, or on a similar blog that links to the podcast episodes… The reason for that is that search engines can't yet search within audio – they can only search words within the entries!

Tip #5

Contact other podcasters!

Once you have a podcast, it doesn't publicize itself! Post your shows online, and contact other podcasters… They will gladly link to you, if they like your podcast's content!

Podcasting is a big mystery...

To most authors, podcasting is probably not of the first rank of concern... First, you might be thinking about the printing of the books, maybe a website, but nothing fancy. Bookstores are your ultimate goal...

However, podcasting, alongside an effective and informative website, can be a HUGE resource for authors! It can drive an incredibly diverse range of traffic to your site, of both new and old customers and fans. Podcasting, if done well, can give you a lifetime of free advertising!

Why should I give things away?

Why should authors give away something for free, when all they're trying to do is sell their books? EVERY person in the internet world is looking for freebies. There is so much to be had on the web for free that it's almost necessary for sites to offer those free things in order to get traffic... Think about which sites YOU visit each day, and you will realize what power coupons, free things, etc. can have!

If you don't know anything about advertising, the fundamental tenet is, if you give something away, you are hoping to get something in return. That worked up until the last few years, when, suddenly, people can get things for free with no hitches, on the internet... But, the new market has realized that, if you attach your own advertising to the FREE stuff, customers will be interested in the actual products for sale as well. For example, if they have listened to your podcast, they will be much more interested in buying your book, and will visit your website for more information! (Which makes it highly important to have an effective website and good handling of your incoming links.) Also, it's your own radio show! You are the host. It's a blast!

MANY WAYS TO PODCAST

There are many ways to podcast, from free to very expensive. But, most importantly, your readers and listeners just want to hear your voice and your story!

All it takes is a headset (as cheap as ten bucks) and a podcasting program (could be free, could get very expensive)…

You can be a novice, or a total tech geek… You WILL be able to do it! We work with many authors who have become podcasters! (Not just the internet-savvy, young, or computer literate – it's truly possible for anyone!)

It is very important that you host the podcast on your own site, if you can, to attract attention to your site (and book) as well as your podcast. Contact us for more tips at 1-866-389-1482.

Your podcast can be very effective advertising – driving hundreds or thousands of listeners to your site and towards your products every month! And, after set-up, it's completely free to update and maintain!

WHAT IS PODCASTING?

Podcasting, simply, is like a beautiful cross between a radio program and a magazine subscription. Once you subscribe, the podcast will be automatically downloaded to your computer in the form of an mp3 – and you can then listen to it on your ipod, your computer, or even your telephone.

With nearly every household in the country owning an ipod or other mp3 playing device, and with ever-expanding use of broadband or cable connections, it has become possible for nearly everyone to download mp3s from the internet. With simple 'enclosures,' podcast playing programs can be anything from interactive Flash players to little old-time radios on the computer screen, and turn all of the podcast creators into DJs for thousands of listeners!

Podcasts have been greatly influential in recent political elections, as well as in the music industry, in advertising, and for the media. Nearly everyone has the opportunity to make their own podcast now. But just how long has this been the case?

BRIEF HISTORY OF PODCASTING:

Podcasting is unique because of its 'syndication feed enclosures,' which are still very young in people years (and in late tweens in cyber-years!).

In October 2000, Tristan Louis, a French blogging pioneer born in 1971, first proposed this concept, using the concept of RSS feeds that Dave Winer, born in 1955, and the author of www.scripting.com, a blog since 1997, had recently developed. Dave Winer then 'enclosed' a Grateful Dead song in his blog on January 11th, 2001. This blog entry was the first true 'podcast.'

It wasn't until October of 2003, when Adam Curry, another blogging pioneer and MTV personality, offered a program on his blog that would, though somewhat imperfectly, sync mp3 files onto an ipod. He tried to convince other developers to build similar scripts. After a lawsuit and other growing pains, Apple got on board with the concept, and developed podcasts into itunes (in June 2005), and thousands of others have developed software launched by the simple concept of the 'enclosure.'

WHY WE LOVE PODCASTING:

Podcasting represents pure freedom of speech. Uncensored, unrelenting, private. Free of spam – you only subscribe to the podcasts you like – there is no way that they can subscribe you! And, best of all: Free of Cost! There are a few podcasts that cost a bit of money, some of which are available through itunes, but usually, those are packaged as video or audio programs, and weren't created as podcasts. Podcasts are designed to be free.

Getting the Gadgets you Need!

Podcasting is accessible to everybody. All it takes is a few tools!

FIRST, what you need is a Podcast Reader, a type of Feed Reader. 'Feeds' are RSS, or syndicated feeds – they get 'fed' to your computer or ipod like a magazine subscription, and anything attached to them (or 'enclosed') gets fed along with them, so that you can simply turn on your device and read it or listen to it!

Podcast Readers are special devices that are meant especially for Podcasts, (Weblog Feeds that have sound attached to them!). Some of the Readers can only be accessed from the internet, and others can be downloaded, so that you can access the material from your home computer, mp3 player, cellphone, or any other compatible device! The downloaded programs have to communicate with the internet, so it is better if you have a broadband connection. Music is very large if you only have a dial-up connection! It will still work, but it will take much longer to upload and download your music clips.

A list of online podcast readers can be found in Note A (at the conclusion of this chapter). A list of downloadable podcast aggregators for Windows and Mac are in Note B.

SECOND, you will find many, many directories online, each one chock full of podcasts. Go to those sites online and find your favorite podcasts, or perhaps podcasts that are similar to the podcast you would like to create. (Sizing up the competition is ALWAYS a good idea!)

Look in Note C for a fairly comprehensive list of podcast directories online!

THEN:

What you need to record your podcast at home:

1) A Microphone.

If you tend to be the kind of person that always buys the best of the best, then all power to you. But it's not necessary! In your research of podcasts (above), listen to the sound quality of most of them – not that stellar, honestly… There are a few 'professional' podcasts that spend thousands of dollars on their intros and background tracks and all of that. But that's not podcasting anymore! At that point, it's become commercialized.

PODCASTING MADE SIMPLE

**You only need your voice, and a topic that
you are passionate about!**

The simplest, most inexpensive microphone options:
   a. A standard headset, preferably with a USB connectivity
   b. A desktop microphone that plugs into your PC,
      preferably with USB connectivity
   c. Digital Voice Recorder, preferably with USB connectivity

However, if your computer came with a good built in microphone, that might be all you need to get started. If you're not sure where the built in mic would be, call your manufacturer, or look in the computer's User's Guide under 'microphone'!

There are also some online podcasting programs that allow you to call in your podcast instead of record it at home. If it just seems too complicated to organize a microphone and all of that, maybe that is the option for you! See Note D for the online podcasting programs where you can call in your podcast.

If you have your microphone all set up, now you need to have some recording software! That can be any software from very basic to professional. It can also be special podcasting creation software, which gives you special options for including music and doing some basic editing on your files.

2) Recording software: RecordIt comes with Windows. iMovie comes with most Macs. Audacity, for both Mac and Windows, can be downloaded for free at http://audacity.sourceforge.net

But, if you are a beginner, you will probably want to look at software specific to podcasting for your computer – which is far easier to 'figure out' because it comes with extensive tutorials, and should be fairly intuitive! See Note E for some free and paid programs you can use to create podcasts on your home computer.

RECORD YOUR PODCAST

Plan your podcasts carefully! This is especially important for your first episode, until you get the hang of it. Take notes about your show... If you like, you could read word for work from your notes, but usually that sounds contrived. Podcast listeners are excited to hear what YOU sound like, imperfections of speech and all!

If you are nervous about your performance, or if you feel that you need something flashier and slicker to help you in your podcasting adventure, check out www.podcastautocue.com You will feel like a true radio or television personality – reading from your very own computer screen teleprompter!

Plan about 3-8 minutes. You can make podcasts as long as an hour, but very few people will tune in! Simply the mp3 file that people would have to download would take forever to load! If you keep your podcasts short, people will be excited to program you in their mix lists, and to recommend you to their friends! You will also have a higher possibility for syndication! This aspect is much like song length for musicians. If you listen to traditional radio, you rarely hear a tune longer than 3-4 minutes!

Keep your content interesting! Try to be prepared before you record, so that you don't have so many umms and ahhs... And stay on the topic! If you wander, so will your audience!

You can get people to come back if you break a reading, for example, into many smaller segments. Read a little bit each day – people will be really excited, and tune in to hear the next part! Keep them in suspense!

Come up with a great intro for the podcast recording! It might be as simple as, "Welcome to the Blooming Twig Books Podcast, this is Kent, and it's a beautiful day in New York." Or, you might want to fully introduce your topic, or play a song that represents your entry... any number of things. Most importantly, get the listener's attention!

And, accordingly, come up with a closing statement, such as, 'Until the next time you stop by to visit... Have a great day. This was the Blooming Twig Books Podcast, Kent signing off.' This is the most fun part of the job! Make this unique – it will invite the listener to stop by again, or to subscribe to your feed!

SIDE NOTE: There are many services available online for professional podcast production, from start to finish. They custom create introductions, voiceovers, complete scripts, audio books and more! If you don't have time to worry about recording your own podcasts.... If you are interested in podcasts for promotion, and want professionals to read for you... If you want an audio book, perhaps for syndication day by day... You might want to consider professional podcast production. HOWEVER, remember, again, that the world of podcasts ISN'T about a beautiful, professional sounding overdub voice (like the ones you hear on movie promos and rock radio stations). Podcast subscribers are looking for ordinary, average people just like them, talking about something interesting to them. That's the beauty of the podcasting world! So, don't go spending hundreds on something you can do yourself! (Though there is definitely something tempting about that custom intro for your podcast! Check out the services below that offer just that for a reasonable fee...) If you do want professional production, here are a few options:

www.audiobag.com Voiceovers/Intros

www.audiobrite.com Audiobooks, Podcast Production

www.podcastproductionservices.com Podcast Production

www.opuzzvoice.com Intros, Production, Audiobooks

www.podcastvoiceguys.com Voiceovers/Intros

www.voiceoverforyou.com Voiceovers/Intros

www.voiceopolis.com Voiceovers/Intros

www.podshack.com Intros and Podcast Production

EDIT YOUR PODCAST

If you have chosen and installed some podcasting software, it usually includes some simple editing tools. You will see the waveform of what you recorded, and if you click around enough, or read the owner's manual thoroughly, you should be able to figure out how to cut sections out, how to fade in and out, and how to add music underneath some or all of your podcast!

You can also have a pre-recorded introduction that you always insert at the beginning of your podcast. You can 'hire' a number of online services to create a custom introduction for you. They are relatively inexpensive, and might be highly amusing to your audience (and to your jealous friends!). It's like starring in your own movie preview!...

If you would like to add some audio to your podcast, please don't add any copyrighted music without permission! It is illegal, unethical, and not necessary!

There are plenty 'podsafe' audio tracks available online at no or very little cost. Find legal music at the below listed sites:

LEGAL MUSIC:
www.audiofeeds.org
www.kahvi.org
www.magnatune.com
www.podsafeaudio.com
www.uhort.no
http://promonet.iodalliance.com

There's also a fun site that has a bunch of free sound effects for your podcast at: www.therecordist.com/pages/downloads.html

All music and content falls under the Creative Commons License online. This is something you will also want to be up on, as a brand new web author and possibly publisher. Visit the Creative Commons website: www.creativecommons.org/license

Remember, after you have recorded your podcast with any of the podcasting or recording programs, save your podcast as an mp3 file (if you save as another format, it will only be available to limited audiences!) to a place on your computer you can relocate easily! The desktop is usually the easiest, but you can save it to any different folder that you will remember...

PUT YOUR PODCAST ONLINE!

The easiest way to upload is with the plentiful free or low-cost programs available online. Some of those programs are designed especially for podcasting, and others are just podcasting friendly. Find an extensive list of podcast hosts in Note E.

That said, also keep in mind that there are many other ways to upload podcasts that are far less simple, if you want your own domain name for the podcast, for example, or if you want custom design of what goes into itunes! Keep that in mind when you are browsing through the possibilities!

Most importantly, use a site or program that really makes the whole process simple for you. If you are having fun and podcasting at the same time, you must be doing the right thing! Most of the programs have complete 'How-To' manuals. If they don't, search your favorite search engine with a few key words about the program or your question: that will yield more than enough answers in the blink of an eye!

POSTING SHOW NOTES

Make sure to post show notes!   Search engines can't search for audio (yet), but only for key words about the audio.   If you have a blog or podcasting program online, they make it easy for you – simply write an entry along with your mp3 upload, and you have taken care of this, most important step!   Many of the online podcasting programs will do this as well.   If you have a blog as well as your podcast, you can also insert a link to the mp3 file hosted by another program online, and in that way do more publicity for and about yourself!

MARKETING YOUR PODCAST

Once you have become a podcaster, you are not automatically going to have thousands of hits!   Wouldn't it be great if that were true...   But you can GET those hits, you just have to go hunt for them!...   Here's a little information about how.

1) If you have set up your podcast on a blog, (www.wordpress.org is the easiest to use for this purpose, but there are a number of possibilities), there will be a tab before you publish that asks if you would like the program to 'Ping' directories.

'Pings' are very neat.   Many of these programs will automatically include this with your subscription.   It is very important. It is free advertising.   It tells the blogging and podcasting world that you have written another brand new entry!

There are many pinging engines that you can notify of your new entry manually as well.   Our personal favorite is www.pingoat.com (perhaps because of the lovable orange goat they have placed on every page!)

2) In the first entry, you were given the option of visiting Note C for some great directories filled with millions of podcasts... Now you should visit those sites again, one by one (unfortunately), in order to 'add' your podcast to their pages, driving up your rating on search engines, and driving up your viewing audience! Again, free advertising – and easy, most of the time! When you visit those directories, most often, there is a place on the first page telling you how to upload your podcast or blog information. Follow the directions, and that's it!

3) This is possibly the most important step! Make sure to use word of mouth advertising to the fullest extent possible! Email everyone on your list. Tell all of your friends and relatives to tell all of their contacts... Slowly, you will start to build up an audience, especially if you keep your content fresh and interesting!

4) You can also submit your podcast to other podcast hosts and online aggregation sites for syndication. This is sort of like a guest appearance on that person's talk show! Our podcast is one of those sites, developed just for authors. Submit your podcasts to www.humanepub.com/podcast by contacting us at Blooming Twig Books at 1-866-389-1482. We will get back to you shortly! This is a great way to widen your audience!

Spend some time at podcast directories, and just click around a bit (itunes is the easiest, but there are many many feed readers that act like big radio receivers for you)... Look for other podcasts like yours, and look for other subjects that are similar to yours. All online podcasters love to be contacted, so you can probably make a lot of contacts and online colleagues and friends that way!... (And do a great deal to publicize your own podcast!)

AND MOST IMPORTANTLY, HAVE FUN!

NOTE A

PODCAST FEED READERS ONLINE

www.aggregato.com
http://app.lightstreamer.com/RSSDemo
www.beanrocket.com
www.bigbold.com/rssdigest
www.blogburst.com
www.bloglines.com
www.busternews.com
www.busternews.com
www.fastbuzz.com
www.fatcast.com/reader
www.feedlounge.com
www.feedmarker.com
www.feedzilla.com
http://findory.com
www.mediatuner.com
www.metarss.com
www.nearestneighbor.net
www.netvibes.com
www.newsburst.com
www.newsgator.com
www.newsgator.com
www.nuwance.com/newsmonkey
www.odeo.com
http://rawfish7.tripod.com
www.reader.google.com
www.rojo.com
http://rss.plech.net
http://server.com/WebApps/NewsApp
http://soapclient.com/rss/rss.html
www.shortwire.com
www.solidblog.com/~cory/aggro/rss_get.php
http://urchin.sourceforge.net
www.waggr.com
www.webnymph.com
www.webpasties.com/prod_news_scrollers.html

NOTE B
PODCAST FEED READERS FOR YOUR HOME COMPUTER

These are the programs needed to hear podcasts or read blogs on your home computer. If you download these programs (mostly for free), they will aggregate the RSS feed. Translation: They will subscribe to the broadcasts you like – pulling in the newest episodes automatically when the program is started!

FOR WINDOWS
www.apodder.org
www.apple.com/itunes/download
www.awasu.com
www.bitscast.com
www.brooklynnorth.com
www.dopplerradio.net
www.dorada.co.uk
www.feedreader.com
www.gigadial.net/public
http://juicereceiver.sourceforge.net
www.newzcrawler.com
www.newzie.com
www.podfeeder.com
www.podsage.com
www.podspider.com
www.primetimepodcast.com
www.pwopcatcher.com
www.rssbandit.org
www.sharpreader.net
www.thirstycrow.net/happyfish

FOR MAC
http://juicereceiver.sourceforge.net
www.apple.com/itunes/download
www.autostylus.com/newsyoucanuse
www.eastgate.com/Tinderbox
www.freshlysqueezedsoftware.com/products/pulpfiction
www.getxcast.com

www.lifli.com/Products/iBlog/main.htm
www.makienterprise.com/newsfan
www.mesadynamics.com/tickershock.htm
www.mulle-kybernetik.com/software/MulleNewz
www.newsfirerss.com
www.newsgator.com
www.opencommunity.co.uk/vienna2.php
www.openendsoftware.com/slashdock/index.html
www.pheed.com/pheeder
www.thinkmac.co.uk/newsmacpro
www.utsire.com/shrook

NOTE C
PODCAST DIRECTORIES – FOR PUBLICIZING A PODCAST!

www.amigofish.com
http://audio.weblogs.com
www.audiofeeds.org
www.blastpodcast.com
www.blogdigger.com
www.blogexplosion.com
www.bloguniverse.com
www.blubrry.com
www.castregister.com
www.churchpodcasts.com
www.clickcaster.com
www.collectik.net/collectik
www.digitalpodcast.com
www.dramapod.com
www.everypodcast.com
www.experiencepodcasting.com
www.feedzie.com
www.fluctu8.com
www.fonpods.com
www.getapodcast.com
www.gigadial.com
www.gofish.com

www.gospelpodcasting.com
www.hardpodcafe.com
www.hwy777.com/pd
www.idiotvox.com
www.ipodder.org/directory/4/podcasts
www.ipodderx.com
www.learnoutloud.com
www.loomia.com
www.loudpocket.com
www.melodeo.com
www.mirpod.com
www.musiconlypodcasts.com
www.mypodcastcenter.com
www.newtimeradio.com
www.odeo.com
www.omn.org
www.ooyhaa.com
www.ourmedia.org
www.pccaster.com
www.plazoo.com
www.pluggd.com
www.pocketcasting.com
www.pod-planet.com
www.podbean.com
www.podblaze.com
www.podcast.net
www.podcast-player.com
www.podcast411.com
www.podcastalley.com
www.podcastblaster.com
www.podcastbunker.com
www.podcastcentral.com
www.podcastcharts.com
www.podcastdirectory.org
www.podcastdirectory.com
www.podcastempire.com
www.podcastdirectory.com

www.podcastdirectory.org
www.podcastempire.com
www.podcasterworld.com
www.podcastexchange.org
www.podcastfix.com
www.podcastfusion.com
www.podcasthost.com
www.podcastvideos.com
www.podcasting.com
www.podcastinglist.org
www.podcastingnews.com/forum/links.php
www.podcasting-station.com
www.podcastlikethat.com
www.podcastmania.com
www.podcastpickle.com
www.podcastpup.com
www.podcastpromos.com
www.podcastready.com
www.podcastshuffle.com
www.podcaststyle.com
www.podcastzoom.com
www.podcasts.com
http://podcasts.yahoo.com/publish
www.podfeed.net
www.podfeeder.com/podcasts
www.podgator.net
www.podmopolis.com
www.podnova.com
www.podomatic.com
www.podrazor.com
www.podscope.com
www.podseek.net
www.podshow.com
www.podspider.com
www.podzinger.com
www.promopicker.com
www.qpodder.org

www.religious-podcasts.net
www.rss-network.com
www.sahfor.com
www.scifipods.com
http://search.singingfish.com/sfw/submit.html
http://search.yahoo.com/mrss/submit?
www.speecha.com
www.sportpodcasts.com
www.syndic8.com
www.thepodcastnetwork.com
www.thepodlounge.com.au
www.thepodship.com
www.vicasting.com/newpodcasts.aspx
www.vitalpodcasts.com
www.yakkyakk.com
www.youloud.com
http://yp.pcastbaby.com/?id=add_cast
www.zencast.com

NOTE D

PHONE CASTING SERVICES

Most of these are pay service, but they include everything you need! Simply call in your files, and most of them will host all of your entries, and do just about everything for you! Very cool for people that want to save time and headaches!

www.audblog.com
www.blogtalkradio.com
www.evoca.com
www.gabcast.com
www.hipcast.com
www.mobilcastnetwork.com
www.phoneblogz.com
www.voice2page.com

NOTE E
PODCAST CREATION SOFTWARE

FOR MAC
www.garageband.com
www.kudlian.net/products/podcaster
www.profcast.com

FOR WINDOWS
www.blogmatrix.com
www.mixcastlive.com
www.makepropaganda.com
http://www.lionhardt.ca/wps
http://www.industrialaudiosoftware.com/products/epodcastcreator.html

PROGRAMS TO UPLOAD PODCASTS
www.wordpress.org
www.audioblog.com
www.clickcaster.com
www.myrsscreator.com
www.poderator.com
www.podcastblaster.com
www.podomatic.com

PODCAST HOSTS ONLINE
www.audioblog.com
www.bipmedia.com/services/podcasting.shtml
www.blastpodcast.com
www.blogmatrix.com
www.cyberears.com
www.gabcast.com
www.gcast.com
www.godaddy.com/gdshop/pod
www.hostway.com
www.jellycast.com
www.libsyn.com
www.makepropaganda.com/download.html

www.mypodcasts.net
www.pcastbaby.com
www.podbazaar.com
www.podbus.com
www.podcast1.com.br
www.podcastfm.co.uk
www.podcastspot.com
www.podcaststation.com
www.podhoster.com
www.podjournals.com
www.podkive.com
www.podlot.com
www.podshowcreator.com
www.privatedomaindepot.com
www.shockpod.com
www.solidsuite.com
www.switchpod.com
www.twocanoes.com/vodcaster

****

**A note about the resources contained in Notes A-E
Because it's such a long list, and is constantly
changing, it's bound to be outdated even by
the time WE next read this, so if one link
doesn't work, try the next! And, if you need
assistance with this or anything else, please
don't hesitate to contact us: 1-866-389-1482.**

****

CHAPTER 9
Author Blogging

Tip #1

Choose to be a "Blogger"
Bloggers are fond of blogs that don't advertise! Find
your issue or your niche, and stay true to that – and feel
free to put links to your books in the sidebar, but don't
advertise! Then you will be a 'blogger' and not
just have an 'author blog' which will be ignored
by the hard-core bloggers and journalists!

Tip #2

Choose to have an AUTHOR BLOG instead…
All of your readers can get a window into your
mind and hear you read your own writing!
Post excerpts and descriptions to your site!
If you have written a controversial book,
you might want to try to be a "real"
blogger first (see Tip #1!)… For help
or clarification, call 1-866-389-1482.

Tip #3

Tie in your blog and podcast – cross pollinate!
Make sure to have both a podcast and blog, and USE both!
Then, whenever you have a podcast entry, refer to your
blog, and vice versa! Internal linking can drive up
your website's ranking within search engines!

Tip #4

Blog as frequently as possible!
If you regularly write entries to your blog online,
you will be amazed and surprised by the kind of
following your blog can generate! Look at
how effective it is in politics!

Tip #5

Bloggers love to link and form groups!
Look for already existing groups, or start your own!

BLOGGING & MAGAZINES

Blogging is like publishing a magazine, but FAR EASIER!... Anyone who is interested in your blog can subscribe to your RSS feed (which is MUCH MUCH easier than it sounds!) on their home computers!

The extraordinary thing about blogging is that you can write about absolutely ANYTHING and people will find you. If you write about horseshoe crabs, the search engines will help people who love horseshoe crabs find you, through complex algorithms and such... The search engines' crawlers visit your site, and add all of your information to a really big database of words, and if people type in your words, they might find you, if your "rank" is higher than other sites with similar words!

It still sounds a bit complex, but, luckily, there are tons of levels to blogging, and you probably don't have to concern yourself with the upper, and more difficult levels that have to do with optimization and such. Likely, you will just be writing entries online, and publishing them with the click of a button, easier than email. The program itself, depending on the one you choose, will do the rest for you!

If you would like to find out more about the history of blogging and podcasting, check out Chapter 8, and the complete guide to podcasting. Although we don't provide a complete guide to blogging here, we can certainly help you figure it all out over the telephone, and if you sign up for a Standard Plus or Professional Plus Author Package, we will walk you through every step of the way, and make it easy as cake for you! Call us today at: Toll-free: 1-866-389-1482.

Blogging isn't all that old, though it seems like it's been around forever! It was only being dimly developed by the academic elite a decade ago, and is now on the forefront of news marketing. All of the major networks have had to take a crash course on blogging and RSS feeds in order to keep up with the immense number of sites offering blogs and podcasts free of charge to anyone who visits!

Quality is something that is, (and isn't) very important, in the world of blogging. The reason we say both is that both are quite true, and undeniable. Quality IS important in order to get listed by some of the better known syndication engines, or to be picked up by a mainstream media stream. Quality ISN'T so important if you are just trying to connect with your base. If you are trying to be in touch with senior citizens, likely any kind of blog or podcast will suffice. If you are aiming for a young crowd, because of their familiarity with blogs, they will simply dismiss yours as 'nothing special' if you don't have anything to catch their attention (in the design, free stuff, etc.)

The most important reason to blog is that...

SEARCH ENGINES LOVE BLOGS BEST!

Blogging is far easier to start and maintain than podcasting... However, a custom blog can go a long way to create a professional identity on the web, and hosting the blog on your own domain server is IMPERATIVE! If you don't host your own blog, you are shipping all of your traffic out to a free site that doesn't need it! Drive up your web traffic by simply writing these entries – they will route the traffic towards your book, guaranteed!

Call us for more information about the importance of a custom blog – we know how confusing it can be, if you haven't spent much time dealing with, or creating blogs in the past!

Call us Toll-Free at: 1-866-389-1482

CHAPTER 10
MySpace and Other Social Sites

Tip #1

Put your "touring schedule" up on MySpace...
Put all of your tour dates up on your MySpace, and send visitors from your website to your MySpace account to check out the dates! At the same time, they will see a ton more information about you, and all of the comments left by other readers and fans!

Tip #2

Put only the details and pictures up...
...that you want EVERYONE to see! Remember that your account is quite public, and if you don't want a picture available to the world, then don't post it! If you don't want your personal name on MySpace or one of the other friend sites, then register your book's name instead, with a picture of your book as your profile image that everyone sees!

Tip #3

Upload FREE stuff...
Samples, pictures, etc. That's what the social space world is all about – free stuff! Offer a free e-book to everyone who pre-orders your book. Or give them a free chapter or two, to tease them into ordering the full e-book!

Tip #4

Network with other writers!
They don't come find you – you have to go find them! Look for book groups, writer websites... Check them all out, and start chatting with other authors about tips, suggestions, leads, etc...

Tip #5

Put an image of your book up on your site!
Almost all visitors on the internet today are looking for visual content... Text is great for the search engines, but the pictures are what draw readers, etc. to your site, and what helps them to stay there!

Isn't MySpace for Kids?

What is MySpace, and what does it have to do with being an author? Isn't it for kids, or for dating singles?

On the contrary! MySpace and other social sites (there are now thousands of different varieties of similar sites) are incredible, free ways to advertise your book, author tour, and website!

You won't necessarily sell a million books off of your profile – but this is an 'extra' that will drive traffic to your site, and, more importantly, give you life and personality on the web!

Look up friends and family…

Look up old friends and family on these sites – you will find that they are invaluable in 'marketing' your books! And you can check out their friends, and add them to your friends list… At the very least, you build awareness among your friends and family… And you will be surprised at the people that will stumble across your book and profile!

Again, if you don't want to put personal information on those sites, there's usually no need – simply put in all the information for your book, and upload a picture of the book instead of a picture of you! And list your website, but not your email or home address… And you will be safe, and still drive traffic to your site!

The 80/20 Rule

There is a rule in all advertising, marketing and business... Eighty percent of your efforts will fall flat! But, ideally, that last 20 percent will make up for the rest! As long as you aren't betting the bank on having 100% of your venture find success, sit back and enjoy the search for that successful 20%! Try everything, and then selectively weed out the unsuccessful ventures later...

CHAPTER 11
Author Videocasting

Tip #1
Upload your videos everywhere!
There are tons and tons of places you can upload your videos online! With many of them, you can actually see how many people have visited/downloaded your movie... This is great, free advertising!

Tip #2
Post videos to your site, blog, MySpace...
Once you have uploaded your videos to one or more of those video sites online, they make it easy for you to post the videos with their players on your own website... Some of the engines will actually directly post it for you, to your blog or MySpace account! This is a great way to add a bit of flavor to your site!

Tip #3
Email everyone you know – they will LOVE videos!
The videos you upload to those various sites are also easily embeddable into your html emails to friends and family! Some of the engines also give you an email box!

Tip #4
Videos aren't hard to create!
Borrow a friend's digital camera, or get your own! Then, most computers come with programs that can edit together a basic movie, with titles and all the rest – that's all you need! There are also expensive options, but start cheap, and see how you like it!

Tip #5
Doesn't have to be professional...
The videos really don't have to be professional. Everything in the book industry points towards perfection... But these video sites hunger almost for the opposite – you will get a following if your video is unique, and not perfect! People are looking for a human connection!

THE #1 INTERNET TREND

Although videos are the hottest internet trend at the moment, most authors, and, indeed, many others are TERRIFIED of the whole new world that video opens up for their public image! Writers have trained all of their lives to be "real" on paper... What do we do when, all of a sudden, we are in front of the public eye?

The role of author has really dramatically changed in the last several years, with a talk show culture... We must all be prepared for that last minute call from the huge celebrity talk show host of our dreams, saying, "We're flying you to Chicago tonight to be on my show..."

A great way to both prepare for that moment, and to show your personality to your fans and the media, as well as to attract new fans, is to create video content and post it online!

Second point of terror for authors: CREATING the video! Believe us, it's not as hard as you think it is! Visit one of the online video sites, and you will see how simple it is... Simply hook up your digital camera or camcorder, and these programs and sites will take you from there to posting your videos!

People DO watch these! The amazing thing about these video uploading sites is that they have real viewership! Some of the people that have uploaded their videos are now having thousands of people watching their videos each day! Listen for the name "YouTube" in the news for a few days, and we guarantee you will hear it! Search for it on a search engine, and get back thousands of media articles that have trickled into the "mainstream" media from the public video uploading site!

Videos are starting to be everywhere – on cell phones, on music players, on satellite radios in cars, in shopping malls, restaurants… Eventually, we will also see videos on candy wrappers, packaging, and who knows where else!... Get in on this new trend now! People will be able to identify with you immediately… and that might really build and strengthen your following!

VIDEOCASTING HOW-TO

There is also a fairly new trend called VideoCasting. You guessed it, that term sounds a lot like PodCasting, but it's with videos instead of sound! In the same way that television replaced radio in every home, VideoCasting is beginning to replace PodCasting as the most sought after source for the mainstream media!

VideoCasting is very easy with certain software – look at the lengthy PodCasting section in Chapter 8 first… Then, once you understand the gist of it, do some research on the search engines, or on the podcasting sites we provided in Chapter 8, and see if VideoCasting is something you might like to try!

If you need assistance getting your VideoCasting career off to a perfect start, we can help you in the blink of an eye! Just pick up your phone and give us a ring:

Call us toll-free at: 1-866-389-1482.

CHAPTER 12
Author Tour

Tip #1
Don't be afraid to be an EXPERT!
(You ARE what you write!) Look into the mirror a dozen different times, when you're least expecting it, and trick yourself into thinking that you are an EXPERT! It's not hard to do! You did, in fact, just write a book!! That's more than many people achieve in their entire lifetime... Pick up your self-esteem and go for it!

Tip #2
Look for little AND big venues to speak/sign!
When you are looking for places to speak or sign your books, look EVERYWHERE! Even consider friends' houses or businesses! Try small local coffeeshops, bookstores in your local shopping mall... And, try for the big places as well – bookstores in big cities, lecture halls, and more! The more you try for gigs, the more successes you will find!

Tip #3
It might be worth it to hire a publicist!
(or a publicity team like Blooming Twig Books) For the investment you make into a good publicist or team of publicists, you might really not only enhance your career, but support your book release with a great book tour! Never overspend, but definitely test the water on publicity – it could bring your book to the next level!

Tip #4
Have a 'tour' in your area...
Look for gigs at bookstores where you are already vacationing, or in your local area! Do the publicity yourself – it's not quite as effective, but it'll do until you have more to invest!

Tip #5
Advertise your tour on your website, etc.
Make sure your readers know where to go!

SETTING UP AN AUTHOR TOUR

Setting up an author tour isn't all that tricky, it just takes time and a lot of patience! It also takes a lot of persistence! If you hire a team of publicists, that is what they do for a living, and they have already developed the talent of dealing with booksellers and libraries... They probably also already have contacts in the industry!

Most bookstores prefer that a professional publicist contact them, and not the author themselves... You will, however, have a modicum of success taking your publicity into your own hands. It doesn't hurt to try!

If you DO have a publicist or a team of publicists set up an author tour for you, make sure that they do what you would like, and not just what might be good for your career... Choose dates, locations and times that work for you in your present job and schedule! Don't neglect your family, your relationship, or anything else for this! It's not worth the gamble! If you are or aren't successful for some reason, you still need your friends and family to support you!

And, for goodness' sake, have fun! Isn't that the reason all authors love to have readings and signings? Enjoy your time meeting the people that purchase and read your books every day! When you were writing your book, you were always trying to picture these people in your mind, but this is your actual chance to meet them, ask them their opinions, hear their criticisms, field some great compliments! And you will be amazed how your books have influenced them!

Weigh your options carefully. Don't necessarily spend thousands of dollars if it's not necessary for your book, or if it's just not going to pan out in sales... But, if your book has a defined and predictably successful market, what do you have to lose? Look for investors, or invest what you can afford into your future career! Your author tour will be worth it if you MAKE it worth it!

WHAT DO I DO AT READINGS?

Some authors love readings, some DREAD them. But ALL book buyers love them! To see the author in person – what an honor!

Choose your most powerful sections, dress nicely and be yourself! They will love you for it... (And remember to bring copies of your book to sell!)

Prepare a reading of your best, or most unique material, and be prepared to curtail it, if necessary – or choose a few sections of differing lengths and themes, then size up the audience when you arrive before choosing which section to read!

Then, when you arrive at a reading, be regal, yet gracious. ALWAYS treat your audience well, whether 5 people or 500! You never know when someone from the media is there!

The general concept attached to reading publicly is to read monotone, in order to let the text speak for itself. If you want to hear some examples, search the search engines for a few of your favorite authors, and see if you can find some readings (even better, see if you can find some video of the authors reading their own writing!). When you listen to them, listen for nuances, listen for intonation... Then develop your own voice!

Then, when you read your own work, focus on the story. If something is witty, your body language should show that it is coming – perhaps a smile at the corner of your mouth, perhaps turning a bit with your body. The audience will pick up on that, and the next time you do that same movement, they will know it's coming!

When you are reading, the most important thing to remember is that you love this! This is your chance to really breathe life into what you've written!

WHAT DO I DO AT SIGNINGS?

Most bookstores prefer signings to readings. They are also great, and might even lead to more sales, because people have to buy a book before they get it signed!

It might seem simple at first to set up and conduct a signing – but it's imperative that you do it right! The more hype, the better... And, the more organized, the better...

First, publicity is key – if there are people standing in line, waiting to get their books signed, then others will join the crowd! If you are sitting all by your lonesome off in the corner, not as many folks will be interested!

Get posters printed at your local printer, and ask the bookstore or venue to post one on the door... Put the other poster on a piece of cardboard and have it standing up on the table you are signing at, alongside a stack of your books!

There are two ways to have the books there – offer the bookstore a "deal" – you will take all unsold books home with you... And offer the venue a big percentage of each book sale – 40% is a very fair price... Don't let them take more than 55%!!

Then, as you sign each book, make eye contact with each customer, and ask them to whom you should make the dedication out, and how they would like it to read.

And, this might sound crazy, but practice your signature! Make it look elegant and special. Find a special place on your title page to sign, or add a little drawing, or a couple of decorative lines – to make your signature unique and special! If you have ever had a book signed – look to see what your favorite authors do with their autographs!

And, most importantly – have fun! This is one of the greatest (and simplest) joys of being an author!

HOW TO NEGOTIATE FOR GIGS

OPTION 1: Store buys books and has them on hand to sell. When you come for your reading or signing, you are helping them to sell the books...

OPTION 2: You bring all the books, and give the store or venue a percentage of books sold. (This is usually the easiest way to work things...)

OPTION 3: You put books on commission with the store. They stock them, and if they sell, they pay you. If not, they give them back.

In the age of the internet, you would think that an Author Tour would be unnecessary... But on the contrary, because this is the internet age, people find greater solace in PERSONAL contact, and will be thrilled to buy your products...

Let us help you out! We can set up a publicity and/or marketing plan with you for as little as 100 dollars per month. Call us toll-free at: 1-866-389-1482.

CHAPTER 13
Publicity Campaign

Tip #1
Don't spend money on publicity if there's no product!
Don't live in a dream world with your book project!
There is no need to start investing in costly publicity when
you don't have a product to push! (That said, you should
ALWAYS do the inexpensive/free publicity steps
discussed in earlier chapters from the get-go!)

Tip #2
Always FOCUS your publicity...
Once you make the step of getting a publicist or publicity
team, make sure your publicity stays FOCUSED on the niche
or target crowd that will truly purchase your book!

Tip #3
Beware of spamming – Don't do it!
Never subscribe to an online publicity campaign that
participates in spamming. It isn't effective, and it might
be illegal, despite what they tell you! If you have
doubts or questions , call us at: 1-866-389-1482.

Tip #4
Don't go over your budget!
Always watch your budget... Though you should
spend one dollar on marketing and publicity for every
dollar you spent on printing costs, you should also be
careful not to overspend on publicity for a book that
might not earn all of that money back! Ask for advice
from anyone you can think of – it will help you make
decisions about how far is too far! Sometimes
it's hard to think clearly about this
kind of expenditure on our own!

Tip #5
Don't aim for Oprah off the bat!
The most difficult talk shows shouldn't be your
first priority... Try to get small shows first,
and then expand on that!

MANY WAYS TO DO PUBLICITY

There are many reasons and many ways to do publicity. Don't over-spend on this until the time is right! You will hear from many companies that will want to publicize you for a big fee. Never spend more than you are comfortable with... There should be an option that will fit you perfectly – you just have to go looking for it!

Blooming Twig Books LLC has a plan that will probably fit your situation, but we should talk about it with you first – call us at 1-866-389-1482. We offer publicity from a couple hundred dollars to several thousand – and can work with you on developing a plan specific to your book!

Be wary! The most important thing to remember is to have the publicist or publicity company work on your project WITH you – don't let them dictate the publicity that will benefit your book!

DON'T TRUST THE HYPE!

If your publicist or publicity company promises they'll get you on Oprah because another book they represent did, they're not being honest!

Very few authors each year are in the elite of talk show guests... We all think that we might be the next big find for a big talk show – but there are thousands of authors that are paying as much or more than you for publicity, with great books and stories... Getting your "big break" is still 99% about luck...

We all know the old adage that lightning doesn't strike twice in the same place. Though that might not be true with lightning, it is almost always true with publicity – if a publicist got lucky with certain talk shows with one independent author, it's likely that they won't have that same luck again! But, for the rest of their career, that publicist will claim that they got a placement for an author with Oprah, and earn millions because of it!

WHAT IS PUBLICITY?

What exactly is publicity anyway? It's seems sometimes more complicated than it really is... But the concept is simple: making more people aware of your book.

Good publicity requires the repeated calling and emailing of representatives within the media, and online, looking for responses, reviews, interview requests, etc.

Good publicity can take you from the short-run world of 100 books in print to 100,000 books in print, in the matter of a few months! In the worst scenario, you get attention for your book, and inspire a modest number of sales. Most likely, you will get some favorable reviews, some interviews, and have decent book sales as a result of a good publicity campaign...

Is spending 3,000-8,000 dollars per month for a publicist (on your new book that hasn't even gotten off the ground yet) a good move? The Blooming Twig Books LLC publicity team is a great, and more reasonable possibility for your book project. We will work step by step with you. Call us at: 1-866-389-1482.

There are other options... Of course you can do it yourself, or with the help of someone you know locally... Or train a student to work on your project...

Whatever you do, know that you are gambling... Don't bet your entire savings on the success of your publicity campaign!

CHAPTER 14
Book Distribution

Tip #1
Don't hold back!
There are many different forms of book distribution,
from local to international... Look for distribution
EVERYWHERE! Of course, if you are picked up by
an exclusive distributor, this doesn't apply... Otherwise,
you are free to sign with many different distributors!
(Read all contracts carefully before signing!)

Tip #2
Don't be afraid to GIVE copies away!
Don't be afraid to give copies of your book away!
It can really inspire reviews and recommendations
(free publicity!)... However, you might not want to give
copies of your book away to people that would otherwise
purchase a copy (friends and family)... That's a business
decision that's up to you! Weigh all the pros and cons...

Tip #3
Enter all contests and attempt with every distributor...
It doesn't hurt to enter every contest you find, and apply
to every distributor... On the contrary, it can only help
your chances of distribution and publicity!

Tip #4
Once you have a distributor the work's not over!
The work STARTS there! You need to DRIVE demand...
One thing most authors don't consider in their hunt for
distribution – after they get it, they have to make it
count!... The demand can be driven by a
good publicity team and author tour...

Tip #5
You NEED a distributor to get into stores...
But it won't necessarily be best for your book! Don't
spend too much on something that might not really
drive sales! Call us to talk it over: 1-866-389-1482.

GETTING YOUR BOOKS OUT THERE

One of the first questions every author asks us is "How do I get my books out there?" There are many possible answers to that question, from small to large! The smaller answers entail things you can do yourself. The larger answers probably entail a good deal of publicity, leading to distribution.

Certain steps in distribution are simple and necessary... For example, amazon.com is the premier bookstore in the world, and they provide authors and independent publishers a way of selling books on their site easily and profitably (though they take 55% of the purchase price). Other large chain bookstores usually require professional distribution...

There are several steps to professional distribution. First, you have to have a book that looks, reads, and simply is, marketable. (If that is the case, you might even be approached by distributors!) Start in your search for a distributor with Ingram and a few other larger distributors. Then look for specialty distributors that might be interested in your book, and spend a lot more time placing your book in stores! The larger distributors are the best to be involved with, because all stores work with them... But the smaller distributors are much more excited to work with YOU on getting your books out there.

Every store gets their books from distributors. It's just not possible for stores to track down every author of the books they would like to sell... That's where the distributors come in! Distributors buy your books wholesale from you or your publisher, and in turn, sell them to chain bookstores... If your demand increases, they purchase more books from you!

We can help you find distribution as part of our Professional Plus Author Packages... Call us at: 1-866-389-1482

DISTRIBUTE YOUR BOOKS

1. IN PERSON

Believe it or not, the best possible way to distribute your books is still in person. If you meet with people face to face, or they come to a reading or signing at a local bookstore, or if you are on an author tour, you will sell more books than you would anticipate. That store also becomes a loyal follower of yours, because they were charmed by your appearance, and they continue to promote you well after you leave. All of the people that saw you in person also tell all of their friends and family… And the best part, you will get the biggest percentage of any other bookselling option!

2. ON THE WEB

You can get a great deal of publicity, etc. on the web, especially because of the power of word-of-mouth emailing, social site and blog conversations that happen in real time… Post special deals on your books on your website, or in emails, and do direct distribution on the web!

3. IN CATALOGS

There are tons of catalogs out there for independent authors and publishers, on any imaginable topic. If you have a self-help book, look for self-help catalogs. If you have a fiction book, look for new fiction catalogs – or if your book is about the Appalachian mountains, or Germany in the 1600s, whatever the topic, look for appropriate catalogs online and in the yellow pages!

4. PROFESSIONAL DISTRIBUTION

Call us – we can give you more information: 1-866-389-1482.

CHAPTER 15
Advertising Campaign

Tip #1

Don't pay for expensive advertising without marketing...
Don't spend thousands on advertising if you don't
already have a marketing plan in place, and
proven results with certain niche markets!

Tip #2

Start small; test the waters.
With just about any service in the world that you need
to pay for, start small, then build from there... Start with a
couple of small, targeted publications, and see how that
works. Then, and only then, test a larger publication or
website, and make sure you are still targeting your
ideal audience! Ask us for help: 1-866-389-1482.

Tip #3

Aim for your NICHE audience.
Always look for a niche that your book sits within, and
target only that audience, to see how the response will be,
BEFORE you go for more advertising. You never know precisely how any market will respond. You should also take a
sampling of opinion from people within your market...

Tip #4

See what your primary competitors do!
One great clue into how, how much, and when to advertise,
is what your direct competitors do! Look at where their
names pop up in the search engines, and within magazines,
newspapers, etc... If you feel that they are having
a modicum of success, follow suit and attempt
similar veins of advertising!

Tip #5

Try the free stuff first, THEN advertise (there's no rush!)
Use free marketing and publicity methods for a few weeks,
and see what your response is. Then pull the stops out, if
you are finding a good response to your early efforts!

KNOWING YOUR MARKET

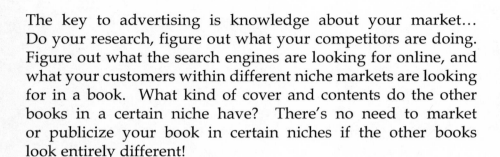

The key to advertising is knowledge about your market... Do your research, figure out what your competitors are doing. Figure out what the search engines are looking for online, and what your customers within different niche markets are looking for in a book. What kind of cover and contents do the other books in a certain niche have? There's no need to market or publicize your book in certain niches if the other books look entirely different!

For example, if your book is on an academic topic, and you have an elaborate and beautiful cover design, (having been designed for a trade crowd), and you don't have a PhD behind your name, your book will likely not fit into the academic book world. Their books look very simple ("scientific"), and their PhDs sit prominently behind their name.

Precisely to the contrary, if your book is entirely scientific (perhaps written as a Master's or PhD Thesis), and has a very simple, academic cover, you will likely have little luck with the trade book audience!

Don't feel bad about any of this – your book will discover its own audience, if you give it a good amount of time... But don't push the book into a box that doesn't fit (the cliché of putting a square peg into a round hole comes to mind here)... Test the waters in several different genres until you find the right fit!

The reason advertising comes at the END of the publicity section is that you should take care or all other aspects first! Try the various aspects of publicity in the order on the facing page, and see how it works for you!

Call us if you need some guidance: 1-866-389-1482.

1. Web presence
2. Free stuff
3. Publicity
4. Distribution
5. Advertising

When you DO advertise, think about the maximum you want to spend... And be careful not to go over that! If you have someone else among your family and friends that you can trust, have them keep track of your advertising and publicity expenditure, and to warn you when you're getting close to your limit! Many times, when authors are wrapped up in their book projects, they get caught up in the apparent success of it, when they are, in fact, spending more than they can ever recoup with book sales... Be careful!

THEN look for the BEST options for your project. If it's a self-help book, look for magazines, websites, etc. that feature self-help... If it's a book on trees for children, look for libraries, children's catalogs, etc...

See if you can get free publicity in those magazines, websites, etc., and after that, test out their classified sections (they are often quite reasonable). If that has moderate success, purchase a larger ad! No rush! With books, you have years to market them as "new" – the market allows this... And even after the books are no longer "new," you can still market them for many years with success!

If you need assistance finding an appropriate publication, call us at: 1-866-389-1482

Part Three:
FREEBIES

Tip #1

Be wary of "free" offers...

Many or most of them have hidden "hitches."
One of the keys to the business is that nothing is for free.
It could be that advertising is paying the site's cost – look
for that... Otherwise, you will be paying in some way,
even though you might not realize it! One very common
way of "paying" is when the site takes your email address
(after you have applied for something free) and sells it to
address lists for spammers... Ask us if you need more
advice about author spam: 1-866-389-1482.

Tip #2

EXPLORE your free opportunities!
Many authors have made it big without spending a penny...

Tip #3

Commit to whatever you choose to do...
Whatever you decide to do, whether it be free or expensive,
give it your best! If you decide to podcast, be a "podcaster"
– you can drive great numbers of new customers to your
site. If you decide to spend money on a marketing team,
give them specifics – a demographic, your niche, etc. –
This is your chance at a new career – make it count!

Tip #4

Ask for help – from someone who knows!
You can always ask for help from people around you that
have more knowledge about certain things... For example –
you surely have someone in your family that knows everything about internet things... Or call us! 1-866-389-1482

Tip #5

Join all and any informational groups you possibly can!
Too much information never hurts! There are groups
online, in print, and in your community! Look around!

CHAPTER 16
(Free) Online Media

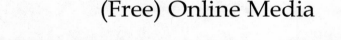

Tip #1
Free is great... for some things!
Although it might seem best to work at the lowest budget possible for your book project, that is not always the case! We encourage you to always think of quality. If you can find a high quality service for online presence at a low cost or free, that's fantastic... But don't sacrifice quality at the level of a few saved dollars per month!

Tip #2
Check out the trends...
Always check out the current trends before you dive into something with all of your energy! Don't build a website that's not on target for what authors like you are doing now... Don't devote all of your energy to a podcast if that's not what will sell your book! And, do some research online to find out which of your free options is the best within the online community today! MySpace is big today, but what will be big tomorrow?

Tip #3
Security is a big issue with many free sites...
We encourage you wholeheartedly to put yourself and your products up in as many public places as possible. However, your personal security is very important, and you should consider carefully what kind of private data you publish online! Don't post your home address or telephone number!

Tip #4
The more the better...
The more sites you can post to online, the better! Saturate your market with information about your book...

Tip #5
Have fun!
The most important thing about all of the online sites and programs that are listed here is that you enjoy posting!

FREE ONLINE MEDIA

Videos, Podcasting, Blogging MySpace and more…

Although there are many options that might be far simpler or higher quality, with small to large price tags, free is a GREAT place to start!

Look back in the earlier chapters for much more information on the following online services. This section is just a reminder that there are many options for publicity and media online at no or little cost. Remember, at all times, these following items can be customized and professionally designed for you, for much better results. But, also remember, that isn't always necessary for authors, and, again, free is a great place to start!

PODCASTING AND BLOGGING

Both podcasting and blogging are quite easy to learn, and very good for search engine exposure. Search engines do, however, notice text, not audio. So, if you have a podcast, make sure to create entries along with the audio that either transcribes the text, or gives notes about the show…

Both of these options are free in many places online, but are much more effective if hosted on your own site with a custom professional template.

MYSPACE

MySpace provides great exposure to a new audience... One friend can easily become 5,000 friends! It is also very easy to join writing groups on MySpace – there are dozens... You will be able to network with other authors and publishers and their MySpace friends!

VIDEOS

There are tons of sites where you can upload your videos – use as many as you can! These are great areas of exposure, and very trendy right now – they are as powerful as mainstream media!

Call us at 1-866-389-1482 for more information!

CHAPTER 17
(Free) Online Ads

Tip #1

Look for all the free advertising you can find!
There are free advertising opportunities in many
newspapers, magazines, and on the internet. Look specifically in the subject area of your book for publications, and
you will be surprised at the number of possibilities!

Tip #2

Do your homework on the competition!
Check out where your competing authors and publishers
are advertising, and what their advertisements look like!
Look up those publications, in print and online, and
see if you can afford the price of advertising!

Tip #3

Focus on your catch phrase...
In any good advertising, you need to hook people
with a few words that will keep their attention for a
fraction of a second longer – and at the same
time give them enough information to want
to check out your book or website...

Tip #4

Point your advertising in the right direction...
The biggest mistake that many advertisers make is that they
don't point their advertising in the correct direction! What is
the point of advertising if people don't go check out your
book, your website, or whatever else you are pitching!

Tip #5

Make sure you have something to advertise first!
Before you go out advertising, make sure that people
will find your book in the store they check out, and will
find your website online (with all pages intact!)

FREE ONLINE ADVERTISEMENTS

Online, you will find thousands and thousands of webzines, newspapers, blogs, podcasts, listservs and more... Just about all of those locations will allow advertising... And they are all also hungering for content. So, of course, try first submitting an article or press release to those online sources... But then, ask them about advertising on their sites... Can you do an advertising exchange perhaps? Or a link exchange?

Some of these online directories and sites are actually specially designed with advertising in mind – they actively encourage authors, or other sites online to advertise their wares, products, and so on! Search for specific sites within your book's genre first, and then go for the more general sites.

Of course, you should also list your products for sale in any store that will take them online – there are many... Look for online "stores" in a search engine, and you will likely run into many possibilities (they are ever changing!)

There are also quite a few sites online that would also be thrilled to have you upload a text fragment from your book, or would perhaps love to interview you for their podcast or webzine... Do your homework, and find a whole list of sites that might be interested... Track them down, then give them some suggested interview questions, or offer to send them a copy of your e-book or paperback to see what they think...

It doesn't hurt to put text excerpts or other information up in too many places online! But remember to always point it back to your site, and to the place where they can purchase the book, or contact you or your agent directly!

You will find a great deal of support and attention in the cyber-world that you wouldn't necessarily find in the print world! Good luck!

CHAPTER 18
(Free) Articles and Reviews

Tip #1

Approach as many possible reviewers as you can.
Reviewers, believe it or not, can really make or break
your book. The more positive reviews you have out on
the net, on the back of your book jacket, and in the press,
the better you start looking to potential interviewers,
investors, book stores and customers!

Tip #2

If you know anyone who knows anyone, start there...
If someone you know has friends with connections, get
on the phone and try to see if you can cash in a favor!
Most huge business deals started just this way...

Tip #3

Any kind of review is great – have friends write some...
Friends are also the best review writers... Have your friends
and family flood the web with positive reviews about you,
on various sites! Or, have the same people send their
articles about your book to various publications online
and print, and see if some of them are picked up!

Tip #4

Don't underestimate yourself or your story!
Never underestimate the value, the strength, or the
importance of your story! You are the author, and your
story has great power and potential! When you approach
the media, tell them about the strengths of your book,
and thank them for any assistance they give you!

Tip #5

Don't give up!
Publicity is sometimes a really difficult process, especially
when contacting the media. Don't give up after one failed
phone call! You will get through sometimes, and it will
be all the more fulfilling because of the difficulty!

REVIEW HUNTING!

What to Send

Send interview questions with every inquiry to the press, in case they are interested in interviewing you! Also send your contact information, as well as your publisher's and agent's information... Send a query letter and a very succinct letter about your book along with a copy of the book or e-book, as well as a press kit (containing the e-book, bio information, pictures, and background information)...

Where to Send it

Send your letters, book and press kit to any media agent that expresses the least bit of interest! If you have not spoken directly with a representative of the firm, you shouldn't submit all of those things! We can all but guarantee they won't answer! Most unsolicited books sent to the media go straight into the trash or the charity bin!

Whom to Send it to

Send the books directly to a person, if you can. Ask for names!

Why Look for Reviews?

Reviews are extremely important to get more reviews, interviews, bookstore gigs, and could lead to much more exposure for your books! Big reviews can lead to big sales figures as well...

When to Send

Anticipate the release of your book by a few weeks, and give the press the exact date, so that they can program you into their schedule appropriately.

How to Send

Send everything by Priority Mail. It looks much better! Submit press kits and free copies of your book, as well as interview questions, etc., to every possible periodical and media source (after you have spoken to them, of course)...

Many media sources will prefer an e-book. If so, simply ask for their email address, and send them a copy of the e-book along with references to your website, biography, etc. But tell them you would like to send them an actual copy of the book as well. Having both copies will help them to single the book out among the rest of the submissions they receive every day... And a hard copy of the book is always preferable, especially if your cover design and layout (and of course content) are attractive!

Also, don't be afraid to ask everyone you know to write reviews – especially if you happen to be friends with or related to any well-known people!

But, even if you don't know anyone who's well-known, you still have a good chance of having a great review written by one of your heroes. If you take the time to write to, or otherwise contact the people you respect and look up to, telling them that they were great influences on your own work (or something to that effect), they will often sit down and write glowing reviews of your work. That could be used for back cover copy, for advertising, for your website, and to use in press releases (which will then be picked up by media sources around the country!).

Your "competition" is also a great place to ask for reviews – they do, after all, know more than anyone else about your importance in the field! Perhaps you can make a trade with them – surely that person also needs a few more reviews!

CHAPTER 19
(Free) Press Releases

Tip #1

No need to pay for press releases...

There is no need to spend money on press releases – there are dozens of places online to post your press releases and have them submitted to thousands upon thousands of interested reporters... If you take care in putting the release together, and make sure it is directed to the right niche audience, you are doing exactly what a publicist would do!

Tip #2

Only trust yourself...

Don't trust another company to put together your press release, or to know who you should be marketing to (unless they are a very reliable company that you have paid to consult with you)... Be strong in your opinions – they are usually correct! But at the same time, be ready to take advice...

Tip #3

Do good research...

The internet is your best library to use as a how-to for press releases. Simply type "press release" into a search engine, and you will receive hundreds of fantastic responses! Type the word "book" or "author" in as well, and you will find some great models for your release! Check out your competitors' releases!

Tip #4

Use a standard format, and keep it concise...

The press release is an art form of sorts – the best ones are very short, and extremely to the point... Again, check out some sample press releases online, and figure out which ones would lead you to purchase the product described...

Tip #5

Make sure it's directed towards something specific

Make sure that your press release is very specific. Target the cities on your author tour!

HOW TO HOOK THE PRESS

People that work for the press all across the country spend half of their time digging through pile after pile of news stories to find that one gem that they go on to publish.

Unfortunately, that stack of news is the chief way to get through to the media on a daily basis. The pile is full of press releases, thousands of which either cross the emails and flat-screen computer monitors of countless reporters each day.

How do you get noticed in that big mass of media?

The answer isn't exactly simple, but with a few weeks and months of honing your skills at this, you will get the knack, and start to see some great results!

First, in creating your press release, do your research! Check out what all of the releases from the big book companies look like, and imitate them, but make yours unique in some way.

Make your release short, but to the point! Don't anticipate that anyone will read more than the first line, so make that one short, sweet, and precise!

Then, as in fly fishing (where you aim for a specific point on the water where think the fish will surface), aim for specific targets within that giant media pile!

Aim for your target genre. If you write about fishing, make sure to include the word "fishing" many times in your press release – it will float to the top if a reporter searches for "fishing."

Second, aim for your target location. If you want to have a speaking gig in your local area, make sure that your area has some key words in the body of your release, i.e. "Tulsa, Oklahoma…"

Places to post your release…

Around the web, there are many free and pay sites that feature press releases, and where you can upload press releases every day. Don't put the same press release in the mix every day – change it, depending on the season, the gig you are looking for, the way you want the media to see you… Keep tailoring the release until you start having feedback of the sort you are aiming for!

Post to your website/blog

Post the release to any territory you own online – your website, blog, podcast, MySpace account…

Submit to other sites and aggregators…

First, ask all of your online friends to add the release to their sites… Then, start doing more research online, looking for sites similar to yours, that might be interested in trading press releases – you post theirs, they post yours… Or, look for aggregators online that are looking for the kind of information that's in your release… Search around on your favorite search engine, and you will find millions more suggestions for, and examples of, press releases!

We can help! Call us at 1-866-389-1482.

CHAPTER 20
(Free) Radio and Media Lists

Tip #1

There are many free radio and media lists online
If you do a bit of poking around online, you will
find many places online with lists of radio and media
lists. Some others you might pay anywhere from a
few dollars to several hundred dollars to acquire...

Tip #2

Look online for contact info of media within your niche
Try looking around online for the contact information
of television, radio, and print media within the genre of
your book! Look for e-mail addresses, telephone numbers,
etc., on their websites – and if you can find them,
names of contacts within the organizations...

Tip #3

Don't approach everyone on the list...
If you find or purchase a list, remember you don't have
to contact everyone on the list! Choose a few key media
outlets that you think will be genuinely interested by what
you have to say and write, and focus on them. Then proceed to a few more, eventually covering a lot of bases!

Tip #4

Pay for lists only if you know what you're getting...
You can find many lists free online, and the addresses of just
about every media outlet in the country as well... If you are
paying big bucks for a list, be sure that you are getting
something great, or saving yourself a lot of work!

Tip #5

Don't give up right away!
When approaching the media, you will feel that you NEVER
get responses... But take heart – that's what everyone feels
like – professional publicists as well. Just keep working at it!

APPROACH RADIO AND TV

How do you go about approaching radio and television, as well as big time print media? As always, start small.

Many places online, you can find radio lists and address lists for radio, television and other programming... If you download those lists (many are free, others cost something), and narrow down the interviewers to those in your genre, you will have a great start!

You can also do your research, and compile your own list of sites and programs that are perfect for the topic of your book... Visit the websites of your local radio or television station and find your favorite editor or anchor. Ask local friends who might know someone who knows that person...

If you don't have anyone you know personally in that station, approach the station via a person you think might be most accepting of unsolicited material – look on the website, in the publication, or on the show credits, for a contact or two that might have clout, but would also be willing to listen to your story.

At that point, come up with a plan – if you make a telephone call, you will most likely get their voice mail. Plan out the call, so that you are covering all of the key aspects of your book, especially those aspects that would be of most interest to that specific reporter. If you email them, provide links to many different places online they can get information and press releases about the book.

Regardless of how you approach the media source, make sure to sound professional at all times, be persistent but very friendly, and search for something in common during telephone conversations or emails. If you are from the same town, perfect. If you went to the same school, perfect – find reasons for the person to listen to you! Once your foot's in the door, the rest is much easier!

Need help? Call us at: 1-866-389-1482.

CHAPTER 21
(Free) Memberships

Tip #1

Join any and all publisher organizations...

There are many non-profit organizations that support authors and independent publishers with information, workshops, special deals, and more... Hunt them down online! Don't stop at one – join as many as you can! If they cost a few dollars to join, it will be worth it for the return of information you receive!

Tip #2

Join writing groups...

Writing groups can be brutal, but they are the next step for any up and coming author. They will tell you what you knew already but were afraid to admit about your own writing... And the best part is, you can tell them the same things about their writing back to them! No, really, in all honesty, this is the best way to proofread your writing without having to pay a great editor! Find a GREAT writing group in your area or online!

Tip #3

Join MySpace groups...

MySpace is a fantastic place to make "friends" and meet people in the business! There are dozens of groups on MySpace specifically designed for and created by authors, with conversations happening all the time about the business! This is a fantastic place to garner support and a whole new base of fans for your new book!

Tip #4

Join Yahoo/Google groups, etc.

Many other websites online, including Yahoo and Google have features that allow people to chat about various topics.

Tip #5

Become a member of a niche group...

Look for organizations within your niche to join!

JOINING ORGANIZATIONS

There are many organizations that can do a great deal for your book, and for your understanding of the industry. Always look out for not-for-profit organizations and groups, because those will be the place that most authors congregate, and the places you can trust the most!

The best groups to join are an uncommon kind in today's world – rooms filled with actual people, in conversation! Writer's groups have been around for hundreds of years, and congregate all across the world all the time! Look in your city or area for a writer's group – you can ask around, and look online, to see if you can find one…

Otherwise, there are plenty of writers' groups also available online, through hundreds of different sites… Those groups aren't quite as good as the in-person meetings, but could be a great way to network, as you can easily be part of a group with several hundred authors, and if your writing is good, you can rub elbows with some great industry people…

As far as organizations, (the corporate kind) there are also tons of them that will give you great tips and ideas for publishing, marketing, etc. Check out our personal favorites – two groups that have an outstanding record of helping independent authors and publishers:

www.spannet.org
www.pma-online.org

Also, be sure to become a member of any organization tied to the subject matter of your book! If you've written a book for therapists, be sure to be part of a national society of therapists. If you wrote a book for children about dogs, become a member of the Humane Society... The memberships look good in your press packet, and they might be a vital resource in your marketing plan!

Part Four:
AUTHOR ADVICE

Tip #1

BE CONFIDENT in your story and identity!

YOU are what people are reading for! Whether you write fiction, non-fiction or something else, the readers are looking for a connection to the author… When you meet them, when you do publicity, when you create your web identity, all the time… Be confident in YOUR story, because that's what they're looking for!

Tip #2

Put out the BEST product you possibly can!

Don't be easily satisfied! Work on the book as long as you can before passing it off to an editor. Choose the best designer and artist you can afford for design and layout, and then publicize and market the book to its target audience. Turn it into the best product you can possibly produce and sell!

Tip #3

Always come up with your budget first!

You should always come up with a budget before diving in headfirst! Or, if you already dove in, come back up for air and take stock of how much you have spent, and are interested in spending! Be careful not to go over budget!

Tip #4

Don't publish to earn a FORTUNE…

Don't count on earning a million dollars because of your book sales alone. That rarely happens, and isn't even really the best thing that could happen… Far better: publish to start a new career!

Tip #5

Enjoy being an author!

Ultimately, that's why we do this! For the pleasure of writing, and getting our stories out to the eyes of the public!

CHAPTER 23
Why Do We Become Authors?

Tip #1

Become an author because you love it!

Ultimately, we all become authors because we simply have to... Most likely that compulsion has a great deal to do with the love of writing, or of the story we need to tell!

Tip #2

Start a new career!

Beyond selling your book, you will be selling yourself... That's a very important thing to keep in mind in this business – when preparing your budget, for example. You will be able to book paying speaking dates for yourself – and that can help to offset book costs...

Tip #3

Market yourself as well as your book.

While starting your new career as an author, market yourself as well as your book. Tell your story as well as the story in the book, because, ultimately, that is what the reader is hungering for – they want a connection to you!

Tip #4

Be careful to protect your privacy.

Be very careful to watch what you put online, and what you put in print media... We recommend against publishing any of your personal data except for your website, and possibly your email address.

Tip #5

Always plan for every situation, success or failure...

If you are successful, what will you do? What if you are on the road every day, visiting a different bookshop, a different gig? Is that something your family would be able to support? And, if you "fail," would you be able to put the pieces back together? Did you over-invest? Make sure to plan for all situations, even if you know (or hope) they will never come true!

WHY DO WE BECOME AUTHORS?

Is it love? Is it obsession? Is it necessity? For some reason, we feel compelled to WRITE this story.

Whether or not it is at the beginning, it BECOMES our story…

And some strange human urge within us drives us to SHARE this story.

And then, only then, do we DECIDE to share this story. At that point, we either sign over the rights to the story we created, or we keep them, and struggle through the brutal process of getting the story out there!

And, only then do we HOPE we could make a living at this!

Maybe even "make it."

But, in that entire process, why is it that we became authors? Why do we subject ourselves to little pay and less respect, in hopes that one day we will receive that monetary reward and respect many times back… And we are hard on ourselves in that pursuit…

And, somehow, we've convinced ourselves, and possibly the world around us as well, that we are writers. Maybe it's just a lifestyle we like, and the book fits that lifestyle. Or perhaps we just had to write this book, and the title "writer" came with it…

Whatever it was, and whatever it is, we are now "authors." We are an odd bunch, full of quirks... But you would be amazed at the things we hold in common.

Most importantly, whether we sell one book or 1 million books, we do this to bring our story to the world. That compulsion unites us.

CHAPTER 24
Why Do We Publish?

Tip #1
Your greatest pride in publishing...
The highlight of every author's career is not, as we might think, the Pulitzer Prize... It's the first time they gave a copy of their first book to their family or closest friend...

Tip #2
Stick it out!
The publishing process is brutal and draining at times, especially if you are working with a good editor... And then, once you think everything is done, you have to deal with publicity and marketing, and it feels like the whole thing starts over! But hard work pays off in this industry!

Tip #3
Focus on quality...
Remember, one of the reasons you are publishing is to create a career for yourself... Make sure to focus on quality with everything you do!

Tip #4
Remember YOUR story
The most important thing to remember is that your story is what got you into this in the first place! Always come back to that story for guidance, and it will (usually) lead you the right direction if you really listen! But, be careful not to over-spend! That will kill the story really quickly, before you can give it a chance to really get out there! Let it flow slowly, moving, like water, into the places it belongs!

Tip #5
Write things down about the process...
One thing that's very important is to take notes about the process. When you are in a spot that frustrates you, pull out those notes and look at all the positive things you've achieved!

WHY DO WE PUBLISH?

Why do we go through the long, often brutal process to produce something that is so temporally small? A tiny, bound bunch of papers with a bit of soy-based ink on them…

It's like childbirth – a painful, long, difficult process… Writing our stories down for posterity, for our children, for society… For the eager eyes and imaginations of the public!

The labor is long, maybe even a decade, or a quarter of a century long… This offspring on paper ferments in our hearts, finally pouring down onto the page… And then, at some point, we reach the point where we have to release the story; where it goes into the world with shape and form.

When you wake up the day after labor is finished, with most of the pain behind you, suddenly, you are in a beautiful new realm…

And then, just as suddenly, another realization comes along… It's not over yet! There is the whole world of online presence, marketing, publicity, sales… You might not have thought that far down the road, and now it's here, and you're struggling to figure out what to do in your book's equivalent to the adolescent years of child rearing…

And then your book starts taking a life of its own – it reaches out to other books, starts to find its own web presence… It makes you proud… And it eventually hits adulthood…

And then you see your story again in a different way -- you make friends with it… You see it for another entity, after many years… You almost forget the process of writing it… It has changed to you, and become something different…

Why do you publish?
Tell us! 1-866-389-1482

CHAPTER 25
Start a Business for Your Books

Tip #1
Hire a reliable lawyer...
When you are starting a business (incorporating), make sure to do it through a lawyer! They have done this a million times, and will make sure that you jump through all of the correct hoops! There are many lawyer services that can save you money if you search around online...

Tip #2
Don't name your business after yourself.
Never name the business after yourself, or any part of your name, if you are in the publishing business. When you publish your business' moniker on the back of your book or on your press materials, customers would otherwise know that your book is being self-published because of the name!

Tip #3
Incorporate or not incorporate?
For most authors, a sole proprietorship or DBA is more than adequate... This will allow you to take checks or other payments in the name of your business, as well as open up a business account... However, incorporation is much better for tax and legal purposes, if you would like to divide your finances between personal and business!

Tip #4
What about taxes?
Taxes will be prepared in exactly the same manner as you have always prepared them, unless you incorporate as an LLC, and then elect to file your taxes as a corporation... Your lawyer or tax consultant will know what that means!

Tip #5
What do I write on the back of my book?
Get a logo made for your company, and put it on the back of your book with your company name!

WHY TO START A BUSINESS

The best reason to start a business, whether a Sole Proprietorship, a Partnership, or a Limited Liability Corporation, is to be able to separate your finances, personal from business...

If you are able to successfully keep your finances separate, your tax accountant will be very happy with you!

The easiest way to handle the finances of a book is to create your own Sole Proprietorship. This is also called a DBA (Doing Business As). It is still YOU, but allows you to operate under a different name – therefore staying separate from your day to day finances! You will then be able to get all of your checks made out to your business name instead of yours, and can open a checking account in the business name.

The only reason to start an LLC as an author, quite honestly, is if you are concerned about keeping your personal and company finances separate... If you are investing a great deal of money in your book publishing effort (upwards of 10,000 dollars), it might be worth your while to become an LLC before you invest all of that money... You can, at a later date, find investors to bail you out, in case your business has trouble, or you can, if all fails, declare bankruptcy without touching your personal finances.

The incorporation of a business under a new moniker quite spectacularly influences the development of your career in a positive way! And the cost is minimal to incorporate a DBA.

You will also be able to put the company name on the back of your book, adding legitimacy to a book that would otherwise seem self-published. Now, though the book is self-published, no reader would ever guess it!

**If you need personal advice,
Blooming Twig Books LLC would love to help.
Give us a call at: 1-866-389-1482.**

CHAPTER 26
How Much to Spend?

Tip #1

How do I keep everything on the cheap?
Start out with a budget, and, in order to stay underneath your upper limits of expenditure, think about certain aspects of your manuscript that need less work, and other aspects that need a great deal of work! Then search for a company such as Blooming Twig Books that can take care of all the services you require, and keep everything easily within your budget (leaving a remainder for marketing and publicity!)

Tip #2

What things shouldn't I skimp on?
Never save money on certain things, including: gorgeous cover design, elegant interior layout, and perfect editing. The rest can be scrapped, as the BOOK is what's important!

Tip #3

Can't I just print the books the way they are?
This is the most common question we get asked at Blooming Twig Books… And, yes, you could just print the books as they come out of your word processing program, with a cover of your own design, etc… But, unless you have experience in the world of publishing, we recommend you at least give it the bookstore test. Try to find a book without the gorgeous layout and cover. Is the Word layout still effective next to that one? Ultimately, it's your call!

Tip #4

You can't bet on selling 10,000 books!
Please, please don't go into the publishing process thinking that you will be able to sell a fortune worth of books… Start modestly, and build up from there – protect yourself!

Tip #5

How do I come up with a good budget?
When you are putting together a budget, think about all of the expenses and time that go into the publishing process!

HOW MUCH TO SPEND?

There are options for publishing from free to thousands upon thousands of dollars...

You don't NEED to spend much at all...

If you are actively able to selectively choose the services that will cover for your book's weaknesses and build its strengths, you can have as much success as if you spent a fortune!

For example, if you write and illustrate a children's book, a little layout work can do wonders... But if you have a rough manuscript for a four hundred page novel, you might particularly want copy-editing instead!

Always remember, it is far better to spend less than necessary instead of more... If you over-spend your budget, you are jeopardizing the most important part of your publishing adventure (you!)...

Don't bet on selling tons and tons of books from the get-go... Test the water with a short-run printing... You will also be able to find all the errors that you would have had to live with for 10,000 copies otherwise!

Contact us for more advice!
Call toll-free: 1-866-389-1482

CHAPTER 27
Can I Earn a Living Self-Publishing?

Tip #1

Should I quit my job?

Never, never quit your day job unless you are sure that you can support yourself OUTSIDE of your book project! It's not worth betting your future on the success of your book… It takes the joy and the beauty out of the process!

Tip #2

Should I invest my savings in this?

ONLY invest part of your savings in this! If you over-invest, you might end up in a really tricky situation, with a lot of books, and very little money to support yourself! Weigh all of your options before you spend any sum – feel free to call us for a free consultation, with no purchase necessary – we can advise about financial aspects, if you need guidance! Call us toll-free at: 1-866-389-1482

Tip #3

Be cautious and ambitious at the same time!

While being quite cautious, don't forget your ambition! That is what can truly turn attention towards your book!

Tip #4

Market yourself as well as the book!

Remember to market yourself as well as your book – think about the book as something that can amplify your ability to give a speaking tour… You are, after all, what you are ultimately trying to bring to the public!

Tip #5

Aim for perfection on a low budget!

You WILL be able to buy perfection on a low budget. Look for the weaknesses of your book, and find the most reason-able ways to right them! Ask us about ways to keep every-thing within a reasonable budget! Call us at 1-866-389-1482!

MAKING A LIVING AT THIS

First of all, keep in mind that it's near impossible to make a living being an author. Even published authors spend little time at home, jet-setting from gig to gig, under contract with their publisher, and earning only a tiny percentage of the profits their bestseller accrues.

However, when you move into the independent publishing sector, it is actually possible to make a living, but only if you allow your book to promote your career! You can earn good money from speaking engagements, and at each one of them, sell a few books... Not that you'll be a millionaire right away, but you can definitely do alright!...

If you want to get to the point of making a little bit of money, you will need to have a perfect book, or as close as possible... That means the cover design, the layout, the content – they all must be top notch! Then, the next stage is marketing it...

Don't over-spend, but don't be stingy in the publishing process, if you are aiming for the stars! Just proceed carefully... Don't gamble your life's savings! And come up with a business plan that works!

You need only as many copies of your book as you KNOW you can sell! You can always print more at a later time... So, focus on the appearance and content of the book – make sure everything is absolutely perfect before you go to press!... And order only a few test copies...

Test the waters, then go for the big run later, once you have proven that the book is selling to your target niche markets!

If you need some help in developing a plan and a budget, we would be happy to speak with you:

Call us toll-free at: 1-866-389-1482.

CHAPTER 28
Can I Get Rich Self-Publishing?

Tip #1
How do I earn a million dollars?
The best way to earn a million dollars is NOT to publish a book! Your chances of earning so much money are very slim! But, earning a fair sum is definitely a possibility, if you play your cards right!... If you are set on making a million, make sure to call us for tips: 1-866-389-1482!

Tip #2
How much should I invest in my project?
You should certainly consider investing as much as you can, while still maintaining your regular daily life... And of that amount, keep about half for all costs after the book is published – marketing, publicity, and the like!... Your total investment could be anywhere from a few hundred to many thousand dollars! Of course, the more you invest, the better quality and greater quantity you receive!

Tip #3
How do I find investors?
If you are interested in investors, that is a great way to support the book. Offer them the first copies of the book, and an ebook before the printing... Look for them any-where, in the form of grants, donations; from friends and relatives, the government, a local arts society... Good luck!

Tip #4
Where can I save money?
That is not a simple answer! Give us a call: 1-866-389-1482.

Tip #5
Keep enjoyment the #1 reason for doing this!
Make sure to always remember that you are in this for the joy of it! If you start basing your writing on money, it just doesn't hold the same significance!

CAN I GET RICH AS AN AUTHOR?

Yes and no...

You can definitely en-rich yourself, and you can find rich opportunities in publishing, though, as far as striking gold, your chances are slim. However, if you do good publicity for yourself as well as your book, you will have an opportunity to start a career as a speaker and author, with speaking engagements.

So, how did that guy (imagine one in your head) get several million dollars with his book sales? How did she (over there) get an interview on Oprah, leading to a multi-million dollar book deal?...

Step out of dream-world for a second here... We all hope to get that big break someday... But you are more likely to win t he lottery than get a million dollars with your book... Not to discourage you from trying...

But, please, please, be careful in your investments. Don't print up 10,000 books to mold in your basement! Don't invest your life savings... Call us up to find out how to save a whole ton of money by checking out the Blooming Twig Author Packages! Or we can just chat about your options!

The big question is whether or not you love this enough to hang on until you find success (or not...)

The great thing is, if you do love this career path, you will find success – it will change your life and make your and your family's legacy much richer! But don't quit your day job until you are sure you can pay the bills! (You are, after all, the most important asset your book has!)

If you find monetary success, that's an unexpected bonus! Don't bank on it!

Ask us for tips! Call us toll-free at 1-866-389-1482.

CHAPTER 29
The Safest Way to Publish

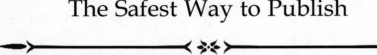

Tip #1
Security is the most important issue.
When attempting to be safe in publishing, keep security in mind at all times! Never publish your home address and telephone number, and only publish your email in certain places (in order to avoid spammers!)... Publish your web address everywhere! On your website, have a contact page that doesn't show your email or other personal information!

Tip #2
Never overspend your budget.
Set a good budget, and make sure not to go over it... You need to protect your personal finances in the process of writing and publishing this book! Otherwise your greatest asset is in trouble (you!)...

Tip #3
Start small, don't take out loans.
There are many, many ways to start out small... Research them, or give us a call at 1-866-389-1482, and you will see that you don't have to spend a fortune!

Tip #4
Make a perfect book.
Perfect is a horrible word... But in the book industry, distributors and chain stores (the target of every independent author) really do expect perfection! Elegant layout and vibrant, yet traditional, cover design... Let us help you find perfection for your book! Call us toll-free at 1-866-389-1482.

Tip #5
Listen to friends and family.
Always listen to your friends and family, about the financial aspects of the book, and with editing issues. Be smart!

THE SAFEST WAY TO PUBLISH

There are many issues to consider in the process of publishing, including, among other factors: cost, quality, quantity, marketing and publicity... We suggest that you stay within the "safe" zone with your publishing venture, and not tempt fate by gambling with your book or investment!

Plan your maximum budget... Then cut it in half... (Save half for marketing later!)

Look at your competition and make a list of your strong points and weak points (Cover design, interior layout, author website, editing, pictures for children's book, etc.) in comparison with them...

Then, find the most reasonable options to get your book as perfect as possible!

When you proceed cautiously with your publishing project, you will likely find moderate success, which can easily lead to much larger successes... But you will also be preparing for the worst, in case your book is a complete flop!

If, alternatively, you over-invested in the project, the entire experience (and maybe your financial life) could be ruined!...

You should also seriously consider starting a business (See chapter 25 for more details) in order to protect your finances, in the case of difficulties!

At Blooming Twig Books LLC, we make sure that whatever package you choose with us is as safe as possible. We don't let you work with us in a way that is dangerous, instead discussing every step with you, and making sure you never go over budget. Guaranteed!

Give us a toll-free call to chat: 1-866-389-1482.

CHAPTER 30
The Riskiest Way to Publish

(Un-)Tip #1

If you want to take a gamble...

If you want to risk more than just the success of your book, then over-invest, print too many copies, advertise in publications before having adequate marketing...

(Un-)Tip #2

If you want to end up in the hole...

If you want to go into debt, DON'T create a budget! Finances can truly get out of hand if you get carried away, or if you listen to the schemes of many publishers online! Take one step at a time, and never gamble on your book! Under-invest instead... you can always increase your expenditure when you see success!

(Un-)Tip #3

If you want spammers to send you 1000 messages/day...

If you enjoy e-mail messages about every possible kind of medicine and part of the body, then publish your email address all over the web! (Use discretion and you won't have much trouble!)

(Un-)Tip #4

If you want people to walk past your book...

Though you almost certainly don't want this to be the case... If you don't like people to purchase your book, you should have a terrible, run-of-the-mill cover design! This industry, unfortunately, DOES judge a book by its cover!

(Un-)Tip #5

If you want your books to mold in your basement...

The fastest way to have your books grow mushrooms in the basement is to order 10,000 of them! Guaranteed!!

DANGEROUS PUBLISHING

THE GAMBLE	THE ODDS	THE PAYOFF
Printing up lots of books	One of 300,000 books printed each year	Slim chances to recoup expenditure
No professional cover design	0% success… (outside of friends and family)	Saves up front $$
NO interior layout work	OK for one-on-one sales, but no distribution	Can be successful with friends and family
No website	50% lost sales on web.	Could save a few dollars a month on website costs
No promotion	1% of national sales possible. Only local sales	Loss of a great number of sales.
Over-investing	Very small chance of making back profits.	Very small % of money invested can get a return!
Advertising (before proven sales)	Small odds of response if no distribution	Small payback on the large investment!

Avoid dangerous publishing: call us: 1-866-389-1482

CHAPTER 31
Inspiration

Tip #1
Stay true to your story…
In this industry, and in the world today, there are many diversions that will come your way… If you are successful, you will be distracted by fame. If you are unsuccessful, you will be distracted by fear… Always remember the story!

Tip #2
You are doing this to help others…
Regardless of the subject of your book, you aren't just in this for yourself! You are making an important connection to other people… If you wrote a self-help book, you are helping people with their problems… If you wrote a novel, you are also, but it might not be as apparent! You are creating an alternate reality for people for a few minutes at a time!

Tip #3
Every author has been in your situation!
When times get hard, remember that every author has been in a similar situation, and that there is a way out!… Take heart, and keep working on it until you finish!

Tip #4
Keep on knocking – the door will open!
If you work long and hard enough, you will open the door to this industry. But be prepared for whatever comes your way! It might be the door you were expecting, but more likely than not, it will be a different color, a different shape… You might not even realize you found and entered the door! Keep your eyes open, and enjoy your discoveries!

Tip #5
Don't lose your love for this story…
Don't ever lose your love for your story, and for your writing! Your audience is waiting to read your every word!

YOUR PUBLISHING ADVENTURE

Whatever you spend,
whatever you devote to this, it's worth it!

Maybe you'll touch one life… Maybe one person will read your story and change…

Maybe your story will put thousands of insomniacs to sleep – your plot pulling them away from their difficult days…

Whatever the topic of your book, this will change your life, your career, and the way the world looks at you!

Enjoy it! This is a great adventure!

Tell us your story.

Call us toll free at 1-866-389-1482.

Part Five:
BLOOMING TWIG BOOKS LLC

Look in the back of this book for special coupons...

Tip #1

We work WITH you on developing YOUR concept!
We spend most of our time on the telephone talking with
people about the options that will best suit their needs…
We create Author Packages around our individual clients…
We don't try to fit you into one of our pre-sized
boxes! Call us at 1-866-389-1482.

Tip #2

We EXPLAIN anything, at ANY time…
You can call or write to us anytime, and we will get back
to you with an explanation – of questions you have about
the industry or anything else having to do with the
confusing maze of the publishing world!

Tip #3

We customize all Author Packages to your needs…
We have unlimited possibilities available for our Author
Packages… From simple publishing packages to
packages including audio books, websites and
more, we run the gamut of options!

Tip #4

We match or beat the rates of all of our competitors!
We will match prices of our competitors for
all comparable services – try us!

Tip #5

We do PROFESSIONAL work at an AFFORDABLE price.
We do extremely high quality work at a price that any
author can afford… We are able to do that because of our
Author Packages – we do much of the work in house,
and can bring the total price down because of that!
Call us at 1-866-389-1482 to find out more!

CHAPTER 32
What We Offer

WHAT WE OFFER

Blooming Twig Books LLC offers a range of products and services, from simple to professional. We are happy to work with each author on custom options, and have developed a service that is able to work on just about every aspect of the publishing industry at the highest level of professional!

We will match our competitors' published rates for our raw services, and we have the rock-bottom lowest rates for professional and standard Author Packages in the business! From a few hundred dollars to many thousand, our Author Packages are the choice for every variety of author, from novice to experienced.

The options available with our Author Packages are too many to mention, but here are a few of note: custom website, blog, and podcast, complete publishing options, from hardcover to die-cut trade paperback, complete design and layout, flash and traditional e-book design and production, book printing, marketing, online sales, publicity and more!

All of our packages and rates are fully customizable to your specifications and needs! We are able to incorporate both tradition and unique style into our work with you, and will be happy to work with you on developing your ideas.

The most important part of our service is the way we bend over backwards to always be available for your needs! Anytime you email or call, you will receive an answer!

We have a dedication to quality here at Blooming Twig Books, and would love to speak with you about your book project! We would love to hear from you! Call us: 1-866-389-1482.

CHAPTER 33
What Others Offer

WHAT OTHERS OFFER

What you get from other self-publishers:
> PRINTING
> COVER DESIGN
> INTERIOR LAYOUT DESIGN
> COPY EDITING (Though very expensive)
> CONTENT EDITING (Though very expensive)

Then, from other sites, you can find:
> WEBSITES
> BLOGGING AND PODCASTING TOOLS
> OTHER WEB STUFF
> MARKETING AND PUBLICITY

Blooming Twig Books LLC offers all of the above, at rates our competition can't believe or match... And, we keep you involved in the entire process!

Call Blooming Twig Books toll-free at: 1-866-389-1482

CHAPTER 34
What Blooming Twig Books Does Best

WHAT WE DO BEST

We are authors working for you...

We don't simply treat you as "normal" clients. We truly care about your book and project, and help you to meet your needs within your budget!

With our Author Packages, we turn you into a professional and give you the TOOLS you need to make your book SHINE!

We offer everything in one big package. No worries about this company to get this, and this other one for the other service... We can provide all of the services at one time, in one place, at a price you could never beat... And on top of that, professional service that will put your book onto the front rack of bookstores!

We offer everything from marketing and publicity packages to Audio Books, E-Books, Online Sales, websites, custom blogs and podcasts, as well as the traditional hardcover and trade paper-back books! Something else you can think of? Ask us about it, we probably offer it, or would be happy to work on it for you!

We guarantee we will always be honest with you.

We call ourselves the Humane Publisher for a reason – we treat you the way we wish we would have been treated as authors!

OUR GOAL = YOUR SUCCESS

BLOOMING TWIG BOOKS
AUTHOR PACKAGES

A brief orientation:

Our Author Packages can be completely customized, from top to bottom, and can also be modified (squeezed, pushed and pulled) to fit within your budget…

On the following pages, you'll see our three kinds of Author Packages, from basic to professional (Standard, Standard Plus, and Professional Plus)

We DO offer individual services of many kinds – for that, check out our rates list.

Contact us toll-free at: 1-866-389-1482

CHAPTER 35
Standard Author Package

STANDARD AUTHOR PACKAGE

The Standard Author Package is our most reasonably-priced package, and comes with a range of basic services, including either or both e-book and book printing.

We also do cover artwork and design and work on a cursory layout (depending on the price level).

$149.00	$349.00	$499.00
Author Page	Author Page	Author Page
Online Sales	Online Sales	Online Sales
Author Rights	Author Rights	Author Rights
Book Evaluation	Book Evaluation	Book Evaluation
	E-Book	E-Book
		Book Printing
		ISBN Number
		Bar Code

Contact us at 1-866-389-1482 to find out more!

CHAPTER 36
Standard Plus Author Package

STANDARD PLUS AUTHOR PACKAGE

The Standard Plus Author Package is for authors wanting to break into the professional side of the industry! From books and e-books to websites, cover design, interior layout, online sales…

$995.00	$1995.00	$2995.00
Book Printing	Book Printing	Book Printing
E-Book Edition	E-Book Edition	E-Book Edition
Manuscript Evaluation	Manuscript Evaluation	Manuscript Evaluation
Author Retains All Rights	Author Retains All Rights	Author Retains All Rights
ISBN Number/ Bar Code	ISBN Number/ Bar Code	ISBN Number/ Bar Code
Online Sales	Online Sales	Online Sales
	Cover Design/ Interior Layout	Cover Design/ Interior Layout
		Author Website/ Custom Blog

Contact us toll-free at: 1-866-389-1482!

CHAPTER 37
Professional Plus Author Package

PROFESSIONAL PLUS AUTHOR PACKAGE

The Professional Plus Author Package is the ULTIMATE author package for beginning AND seasoned professional authors!

$4000	$5500	$7000
Author Website	Author Website	Author Website
Custom Blog	Custom Blog	Custom Blog
Author Podcast	Author Podcast	Author Podcast
Book Printing	Book Printing	Book Printing
Copy Editing	Copy Editing	Copy Editing
E-Book Edition	E-Book Edition	E-Book Edition
Cover Design	Cover Design	Cover Design
Interior Layout	Interior Layout	Interior Layout
ISBN Number	ISBN Number	ISBN Number
Bar Code	Bar Code	Bar Code
Author Page	Author Page	Author Page
Online Sales	Online Sales	Online Sales
Author's Rights	Author's Rights	Author's Rights
Manus. Evaluation	Manus. Evaluation	Manus. Evaluation
Market. Resources	Market. Resources	Market. Resources
	Press Release	Press Release
	CD-Rom Press Kit	CD-Rom Press Kit
	Publicity Toolkit	Publicity Toolkit
		Audio Book

CHAPTER 38
Author Package Comparison Chart

AUTHOR PACKAGE COMPARISON

Standard Package	Std. Plus Package	Prof. Plus Pkg.
	Author Website	Author Website
	Custom Blog	Custom Blog
		Author Podcast
Book Printing	Book Printing	Book Printing
		Copy Editing
E-Book Edition	E-Book Edition	E-Book Edition
	Cover Design	Cover Design
	Interior Layout	Interior Layout
ISBN Number	ISBN Number	ISBN Number
Bar Code	Bar Code	Bar Code
Author Page	Author Page	Author Page
Online Sales	Online Sales	Online Sales
Author's Rights	Author's Rights	Author's Rights
Manus. Evaluation	Manus. Evaluation	Manus. Evaluation
		Market. Resources
		Press Release
		CD-Rom Press Kit
		Publicity Toolkit
		Audio Book

Contact us toll-free at: 1-866-389-1482!

BLOOMING TWIG RATE LIST

At Blooming Twig Books LLC, we also offer some of the most competitive rates in the industry for professional service and products for authors! If you decide not to accept an Author Package deal, you will find what you need in the rate list!

From book printing to e-book design, custom blogs and podcasts to easily updated author websites, 25 copies of your book to ten thousand, we can find the custom solution for you!

If you find a lower advertised rate somewhere on the web, it would be our pleasure to match it for you! Try us out!

We can also work on custom options for your project – simply tell us what you are trying to do, and if we can't do it, we will give you our best advice as to where you can get the best service at the lowest affordable price! Guaranteed!

For more up to date rates, with more specifics, give us a toll-free call at: 1-866-389-1482… We can't wait to hear from you!

CHAPTER 39
Blooming Twig Book Printing

Copies (4"X7")	Price	Price/Copy
25	$250	$10.00
50	$400	$8.00
100	$550	$5.50
200	$900	$4.50
500	$2000	$4.00

Copies (6"X9")	Price	Price/Copy
25	$300	$12.00
50	$475	$9.50
100	$750	$7.50
200	$1200	$6.00
500	$2500	$5.00

Copies (8.5"X11")	Price	Price/Copy
25	$375	$15.00
50	$600	$12.00
100	$1000	$10.00
200	$1700	$8.50
500	$3750	$7.50

(The above quotes are based on softcover books of 100 pages)
Call for prices on Children's Books, all Hardcover printing,
and all orders greater than 500 copies,
or books of more than 100 pages!
Toll-Free: 1-866-389-1482

CHAPTER 40
Blooming Twig E-Books

E-BOOK EDITIONS

We regularly offer two kinds of E-Books, offered for sale in our online store, as well as on our clients' websites. The PDF E-Book is a simple solution that is most widely used, but far less protected. Our specialty Flash E-Books are fully protected by Flash technology, and are highly interactive...

OPTIMIZED PDF E-BOOK	$495.00+
SECURE FLASH E-BOOK	$295.00+

Contact Blooming Twig Books for more information on our E-Book Editions:

Toll-Free: 1-866-389-1482

CHAPTER 41
Blooming Twig Cover Design and Interior Layout Design

COVER DESIGN/INTERIOR LAYOUT

	By the Hour	By the Project
Cover Design	$170/hr.	$295.00+
Cover Artwork	$225/hr.	$349.00+
Interior Design	$130/hr.	$4-7.50 per page
Interior Artwork	$225/hr.	$349.00+

Call us for more information:
Toll-free: 1-866-389-1382

CHAPTER 42
Blooming Twig Copy and Content Editing

COPY EDITING

Pages	Single Edit	Multiple Edits
0-25 pages	$5.00 per page	$8.00 per page
26-50 pages	$4.50 per page	$7.50 per page
51-100 pages	$4.00 per page	$7.00 per page
101-200 pages	$3.50 per page	$6.50 per page
201+ pages	$3.00 per page	$6.00 per page

Editing is included with some
Author Packages. Ask us!

Call us for more information:
Toll-free: 1-866-389-1382

CHAPTER 43
Blooming Twig Author Websites

AUTHOR WEBSITES

BASIC HTML WEBSITE
Price: $395.00+ (or $130/hr.)
Included with Certain Author Packages

PROFESSIONAL HTML WEBSITE
Price: $95+ (or $130/hr.)
Included with Certain Author Packages

FLASH WEBSITE
Price: $495+ (or $170/hr.)
Included with Certain Author Packages

AMERICAN AUTHOR WEBSITE
Price: $299+
Included with Certain Author Packages.

*We offer specialty Author Websites through our
friends at American Author websites (americanauthor.com), and
would be happy to include one of their sites in your
package deal... Otherwise, sign up with them directly,
and tell you Blooming Twig Books sent you!*

Contact us for more information! 1-866-389-1482

CHAPTER 44
Blooming Twig Author
Blogs and Podcasts

PERSONALIZED BLOG/PODCAST

CUSTOMIZED BLOG
Price: $295.00+ (or $130/hr.)
Included with Certain Author Packages

CUSTOM BLOG *(if you purchased a website through Blooming Twig Books)*
Price: $95+ (or $130/hr.)
Included with Certain Author Packages

PERSONALIZED PODCAST
Price: $350+ (or $130/hr.)
Included with Certain Author Packages

CUSTOM PODCAST *(if you purchased a website through Blooming Twig Books)*
Price: $125+ (or $130/hr.)
Included with Certain Author Packages

There are many options out there for blogs and podcasts. Blooming Twig Books LLC offers fully customized solutions, especially made for your needs...

Call us for more details! Toll-Free 1-866-389-1482

CHAPTER 45
Blooming Twig Author
Publicity Packages

BLOOMING TWIG BOOKS PUBLICITY

PUBLICITY TOOL KIT
Price: $995
Included with Certain Author Packages

CD/MEDIA PRESS KIT
Price: $895
Included with Certain Author Packages

PRESS RELEASE AND DISTRIBUTION
Price: $595
Included with Certain Author Packages

*We also offer specialized options for publicity
with our publicity team at Blooming Twig Books.
We charge either by the hour, or by the month,
depending on which is more reasonable for you!*

*We can do any level of publicity you
need, in every price range!*

*Call us for more information!
Toll-free: 1-866-389-1482*

ABOUT BLOOMING TWIG BOOKS

Blooming Twig Books LLC
3A Detmer Road
East Setauket, NY 11733

Telephone, Toll-Free: 1-866-389-1482
Telephone: 1-631-612-2090
Fax: 1-631-389-2607

Email Blooming Twig Books:
info@bloomingtwigbooks.com

Email Kent S. Gustavson:
kent@bloomingtwigbooks.com

Visit us online:
www.bloomingtwigbooks.com

Author Packages:
www.bloomingtwigbooks.com/packages.html

Author Rates:
www.bloomingtwigbooks.com/rates.html

Blooming Twig Books LLC Philosophy:
www.bloomingtwigbooks.com/philosophy.html

Visit our online Book Shop!
www.bloomingtwigbooks.com/shop

ABOUT THE EDITOR

Kent S. Gustavson is the founder of Blooming Twig Books LLC, and still answers most of the phone calls… He is also a multi-talented editor, agent and artist.

He lives in New York with his smart, witty and beautiful fiancé, and is a PhD musician, composer, author, teacher, and ne'er- do-well. His family lives in Oklahoma, but he grew up on the open range of Minnesota and in the dense humidity of Louisiana.

He has a dozen or more albums out on Ninety and Nine Records (www.ninetyandninerecords.com) and a couple of other labels, as well as many classical scores and the like. Check out his music website at www.kentgustavson.com

Contact him directly at:

kent@bloomingtwigbooks.com

THE HUMANE PUBLISHER
WRITING CONTEST

GRAND PRIZE
Free Blooming Twig Books
Professional Plus Publishing Package
($4,000.00 value*)

FIRST PRIZE IN EACH CATEGORY
Free Ipod Shuffle (for your podcasts)
AND 25% off Professional Plus Author Package

SECOND PRIZE IN EACH CATEGORY
25% off Professional Plus Author Package

FINALISTS IN ALL CATEGORIES
will also be acknowledged publicly.

*See www.bloomingtwigbooks.com/packages.html

THE HUMANE PUBLISHER
WRITING CONTEST

SELF-HELP/THERAPY

POETRY

MIND, BODY, SPIRIT/SPIRITUAL

NON-FICTION

FICTION

To Enter, please send your complete manuscript to:

HUMANE PUBLISHER CONTEST
BLOOMING TWIG BOOKS LLC
3A DETMER ROAD
EAST SETAUKET, NY 11733

Include a check for $35.00 made out to
Blooming Twig Books. You may also
call to pay: 1-866-389-1482.

Make sure to include your e-mail address, so that you can be
notified when the contest winners have been chosen! Submit
the form on the following page along with your manuscript.
Please, no other cover letters or anything else! Good luck!
Contact us for the contest entry deadlines.

(Either tear this page out of the book and send it to us, or email us at info@bloomingtwigbooks.com with all of your information!)

Contest Entry Form

Name: ______________________________

Address: ______________________________

____

Email: ______________________________

Title of your entry: ______________________________

Category of your Entry (circle one):

Fiction
Non-Fiction
Self-Help/Therapy
Poetry Collection
Mind, Body, Spirit/Spiritual

$35.00 Entry Fee Required (See Previous Page)

SPECIAL COUPONS

PROFESSIONAL PLUS PACKAGE COUPON
15% off Professional Plus Package
Bonus: Ipod Video (to store your podcasts!)
(approx. 900-1400 dollar total value! Non-transferable, not good with other coupons, expiration 5/31/2008)

STANDARD PLUS PACKAGE COUPON
15% off Standard Plus Package
Bonus: Ipod Nano (to store your podcasts!)
(approx. 400-600 dollar total value! Non-transferable, not good with other coupons, expiration 5/31/2008)

STANDARD PACKAGE COUPON
15% off Standard Package, and
bonus: Ipod Shuffle (to store your podcasts!)
(approx. 110-250 dollar total value! Non-transferable, not good with other coupons, expiration 5/31/2008)

RATES COUPONS
> 10% discount on book printing
> 50% discount on design services
> 50% discount on e-books
> Ask us about the rest!

(Non-transferable, not good with other coupons, expiration 5/31/2008)

CUSTOMER'S CHOICE COUPON
This coupon is a "Customer's Choice" Coupon. It gives you free license to "bargain" with us on your own, customized package deal...
(Non-transferable, not good with other coupons, expiration 5/31/2008)